Writers of Wales

Rhys Davies

Editors:

Meic Stephens

Jane Aaron

M. Wynn Thomas

Honorary Series Editor:

R. Brinley Jones

Writers of Wales

Rhys Davies

Huw Edwin Osborne

University of Wales Press

Cardiff 2009

© Huw Edwin Osborne, 2009

All rights reserved. No part of this book may be reproduced in any material form (including photocopying or storing it in any medium by electronic means and whether or not transiently or incidentally to some other use of this publication) without the written permission of the copyright owner except in accordance with the provisions of the Copyright, Designs and Patents Act 1988 or under the terms of a licence issued by the Copyright Licensing Agency Ltd, Saffron House, 6–10 Kirby Street, London, EC1N 8TS. Applications for the copyright owner's written permission to reproduce any part of this publication should be addressed to The University of Wales Press, 10 Columbus Walk, Brigantine Place, Cardiff, CF10 4UP.

www.uwp.co.uk

British Library Cataloguing-in-Publication Data
A catalogue record for this book is available from the British Library.

ISBN 978-0-7083-2167-6
e-ISBN 978-0-7083-2242-0

The right of Huw Edwin Osborne to be identified as author of this work has been asserted by him in accordance with sections 77, 78 and 79 of the Copyright, Designs and Patents Act 1988.

Printed in Wales by Dinefwr Press, Llandybïe

Contents

Acknowledgements	iv
Abbreviations	vi
Introduction	1
1 Little Lord Fauntleroy of the Valleys	7
2 'A rainbow wash of the mind'	16
3 A bohemian in Grub Street	26
4 A 'professional Welshman'	36
5 A 'natural amusing greed'	42
6 A curious friendliness among the men	50
7 'The raw stuff of life'	58
8 'Time and the Welsh mountains'	68
9 'Strange embraces' and 'subtle pagan secrets'	76
10 'One's own interior liberty'	84
11 'Down with passports to art'	96
12 Dealing in dark murders	104
13 A 'borderline case'	123
Conclusion	132
Bibliography	136
Index	143

Acknowledgements

I owe a particularly heavy debt of gratitude to Dr Gary Kelly for his invaluable guidance and mentoring when I began researching Rhys Davies as a Ph.D. candidate at the University of Alberta. I am also grateful to Dr Patricia Rae and Dr Heather Zwicker for their long-term and enthusiastic support of and interest in my work. Thanks are also due to the many friends and colleagues, including everyone here in the Department of English at the Royal Military College of Canada, especially Dr Heather Evans, with whom I have shared discussions on Davies throughout the years. My understanding of Davies's personality and character were enriched by the recollections of Charles Lahr's daughters, Oonagh and Sheila, for whose time and generosity I am grateful. Thanks are also due to the archivists at the National Library of Wales, the Harry Ransom Humanities Research Centre, and especially to Ali Burdon and Alun Ford at the University of London's Sterling Library. An additional special thanks is due to Jean Rose at the Random House Archives and Library for going so far above and beyond her duties to provide resources that deepened my understanding of Davies's career. I am also grateful to Sarah Lewis at the University of Wales Press for her kind and diligent assistance at every stage of this book's life, from proposal to publication. Thanks also to Emeritus Professor Meic Stephens for his keen editorial eye and for his expert and generous insights. Last, but not least, thanks to Cory for his patience and support. Any faults in this text are my own responsibility, and they remain despite the assistance of these people.

For permissions to reproduce photographs of Rhys Davies, I thank the Harry Ransom Humanities Research Centre and the Estate of

Rhys Davies. For permission to reproduce the photograph of Davies in Final Marina, I thank the Sterling Library, University of London. For permission to reproduce the photograph of Clydach Vale, I thank Reflective Images (*http://www.wales-pictures.com*). For permission to reproduce William Roberts's cover art for *The New Coterie*, I thank the William Roberts Society. For permission to quote from the account ledgers and correspondence in the William Heinemann archives, I thank the Random House Group Ltd.

Abbreviations

ADE	A. Dywe Evans
AG	Arnold Gyde
CL	Charles Lahr
FU	Fred Urquhart
GB	George Bullock
GF	Gilbert Fabes
GHW	G. H. West
HRHRC	Harry Ransom Humanities Research Centre
KD	Kay Dick
HWS	Harry Warren Schwartz
LQ	Louis Quinain
NLW	National Library of Wales
PH	Philip Henderson
RHAL	Random House Archive and Library
RD	Rhys Davies
RG	Robert Gibbings
RCC	Rupert Croft-Cooke
RM	Raymond Marriott
SL	Sterling Library

For my parents, Ann and Brian

Introduction

Rhys Davies was born in 1901 in Blaenclydach, a village in a tributary valley of the Rhondda Fawr in south Wales. There are a lot of geographical qualifiers in this address and, to be sure, Davies grew up in a world of clearly demarcated and fiercely defended microgeographies. It is only natural, therefore, that he was acutely aware of borders of all kinds, both physical and ideological. The borders of his youth, invisible to the visitor but essential to local identities, ran everywhere – dividing neighbourhoods, cutting main streets in half, keeping pub clear of chapel, crisscrossing each mind. Dai Smith illustrates this phenomenon when describing Tonypandy, which is just down the street from Davies's home and which is, to me, indistinguishable from Clydach, Blaenclydach or Clydach Vale:

> The boundaries of somewhere like Tonypandy are indefinable. Those who have lived there will tell you, within a street's length or span where Tonypandy 'proper' began and Llwynypia ended, or where Clydach Vale swoops down to end in the 'grander precincts' of De Winton and Dunraven Street or when you have left Tonypandy and entered Penygraig. This intense delineation of territory is nothing to do with council boundaries, political wards or ancient land grants. It is certainly not to do with a separating, physical sense of place since all of mid-Rhondda, and, by extension, large tracts of the coal mining valleys in South Wales blur indistinguishably the one into the other. What it means is that no one ever actually came from 'the Valleys'. They came from those segments of individual and local experience, geographically delimited by mutual consent, through which the wider bonding summarized by a term like the Valleys is given reality. Otherwise it remains an abstraction, almost a cliché. So, 'Where do you come from?' – once as insistent a query in place-conscious Wales as its follow up, 'What do

you do *now*?' – is defined exactly as a locality whose parameters are known by those who need to know them. Tonypandy was, and might have remained, simply a framework for experiencing social identity. It became a country of the mind. (Smith, 1999: 99–100)

Davies, who was an avid border-crosser all his life, came from a context of subtle division and definition. The borders that Davies experienced were not simply geographical. They were also the borders of 'individual and local experience' that divide places with more subtle and invisible boundaries, be they the boundaries between forms of work, between men and women, between heterosexuality and a marginalized homosexuality, between Welsh and English, between past and present. These are all borders that are central to Davies's life and writing. This book describes how Davies's writing reflects his existence in the in-between spaces of identity; it asks what it meant to live and write at the points where these boundaries, these fault-lines, intersect.

So, while Davies is a 'Writer of Wales', the Wales that he helps us to see is, to borrow M. Wynn Thomas's term, a Wales of 'internal difference'. Davies lived in the interstices of culture, so we must think of Wales not as a geographically delimited space resting safely behind its mountainous ramparts, but as a site of constantly negotiated states of difference. Again like M. Wynn Thomas, we must think of Wales in terms of Homi K. Bhabha's discussion of nation: 'It is in the emergence of the interstices – the overlap and displacement of domains of difference – that the intersubjective and collective experiences of nationness, community interest, or cultural value are negotiated' (Bhabha, 1994: 2). Likewise, we must approach Davies as he is formed '"in-between", or in excess of, the sum of the "parts" of difference (usually intoned as race/class/gender, etc.)' (ibid.). Much of Davies's formative experience occurred along boundaries upon which he existed liminally, never able to settle comfortably into available definitions of selfhood and belonging. So we must, as Mikhail Bakhtin explains, dismiss the 'interior territory' of culture in order to grasp its living texture:

> One must not . . . imagine the realm of culture as some sort of spatial whole, having boundaries but also having internal territory. The realm of culture has no internal territory: it is entirely distributed along the boundaries, boundaries pass everywhere, through its every aspect . . . Every cultural act lives essentially on the boundaries: in this is its seriousness and significance; abstracted from boundaries it loses its soil, it becomes empty, arrogant, it degenerates and dies. (quoted in Morson and Emerson, 1990: 51)

Bakhtin privileges the boundary against the interior territory. He claims, in fact, that there is no interior territory, securely defined within its oppositional boundaries, but only sites of negotiation that intersect infinitely with other sites of negotiation. When culture is simplified from its multiplicity and flux, when we seek to render it static and 'comprehensible', we lose sight of its active reality. Davies is a liminal or interstitial figure in that he could not rest comfortably within the established boundaries of his Welsh experience, but strained against them, operating constantly in their active negotiation.

For Davies was a grocer's son in a coal-mining community; he was a Welshman who left Wales to write about his homeland from London; and he was gay in, initially, a heavily masculine and homophobic context, and, later, in a freer, but still repressive, London. As a grocer's son, Davies lived with, but was not part of, the working community of Blaenclydach. Although surrounded by proletarian forms of life, he was excluded from them by his petit-bourgeois status. Living so closely with a mining community, however, Davies could not help but identify and sympathize with the working life constituting his daily experience. In his writing, therefore, he turns again and again to this community of his youth. However, this identification was never complete, not only because of class restrictions, but because Davies's gayness made it extremely difficult to live within the oppressively masculine nature of working-class male culture. As Wales was increasingly defined by the densely populated industrial South and its working communities, Davies had to look beyond the borders of Wales to find an accommodating context for an identity that did not conform to the dominant forms of life in which he grew up. In desperation, he turned to writing and to London, but continually returned to Wales as the primary setting for his stories and novels.

Davies presents himself as a mobile border figure in an unpublished autobiographical sketch where he outlines his dislikes, which include 'Taking a lease of a house or flat. The prospect of settling anywhere. The thought of frontiers becoming difficult to cross. Hospitals. Prisons' (NLW MS 20897 E 108 1948). This was a man who feared immobility, containment and confinement; who needed movement and transgression; who lived in transit, spending much of his life going from London, to countryside, to the Continent, to Blaenclydach, moving from flat to flat and having no fixed address, save the forwarding addresses of friends or his publisher. The inclusion of prisons and hospitals, both authorities that identify, 'cure' and punish deviance, is particularly revealing of the gay Davies, and, as this book will argue, Davies never passively succumbed to the disciplinary forces that silenced his sexuality. Rather, he found ways to explore and express his sexuality within the more marketable Welsh and working-class themes of his novels and stories.

Indeed, Davies was aware that forms of repressive power are undermined by the very pleasures they seek to repress and upon which they inevitably depend. For instance, a scene partly edited out from the second draft of Davies's autobiography, *Print of a Hare's Foot* (1967), reflects Michel Foucault's theories on power and repression. Davies revels in a literal act of border-crossing and indulges in the mutual penetration of two pleasures: on the one hand, the 'pleasure that comes from exercising a power that questions, monitors, watches, spies, searches out, palpitates, brings to light; and on the other hand, the pleasure that kindles at having to evade this power, flee from it, fool it, or travesty it' (Foucault, 1990: 45):

> Customs sheds are fairy palaces to me. To this day they are halls of magic adventure. I would not have their guardians – apparently much-detested in Newhaven by travellers' [*sic*] coming into England – thrown

into the harbour. I like their expert rummaging into my luggage and their wholesale suspicion of villainy in the human race. The charm of a trip abroad would lose a Gilbert and Sullivan antic if these guardians were abolished. I always try to select the most blackguardly-looking officer for examination of my luggage. It is a joy to witness a foreign woman, especially if she is French, do her stuff for these cement-faced male hags. A customs shed at boat-time would make a good theme for a ballet. (NLW 21533 C 148)

Davies makes a spectacle of border-crossing and heightens the theatrical and overwatched nature of borders and the differences that they attempt to naturalize. His relish of this anarchic scene travesties authority even as he submits to it, rendering the power of these 'fairy palaces' illusory. There is an almost erotic indulgence in his enjoyment of having his private luggage 'examined' by the most 'blackguardly-looking officer', and of being 'rummaged' by the 'guardians'. His pleasure in submitting to authority undermines that authority even as he submits to it, showing up the whole performance of guarding against differences, and finally casting aside difference and boundary in the gender-bending words 'male hags'. Davies, who rejected the limitations of the Rhondda, liked to play along those intersecting boundaries that Bakhtin and Bhabha describe as the very life of culture.

The book begins by discussing Davies's childhood in Blaenclydach as a negotiation of his queer sexuality within Welsh working-class masculinity and Welsh Nonconformist respectability. It explains how the young Davies was forced to discover and invent an alternative tradition of identification through literature and art, which eventually became the impetus for his escape from Wales into the liberating world of bohemian creativity in London and France. In these early years of Davies's career, he established himself by exploiting his reception as a distinctly Welsh author and by portraying Wales within an English colonialist infantilization and feminization of Wales. The misogyny of this early fiction was one aspect of Davies's repudiation of Nonconformist respectability, but it also stands in opposition to the idealized and eroticized working-class masculinity through which

Davies effected a return home to the working communities of his youth. This return home was also achieved through an appeal to the Romantic Welsh past, which, while pandering to an English market for an exotic Wales, provided a liberating pre-industrial Welsh paganism that mapped a landscape of sexual identification for the self-exiled Welsh queer.

The years around the Second World War, brought several significant changes to Davies's life and fiction. While politically shaken by the conflict, Davies moved away from the working-class Welsh politics that defined the first half of his career. Increasingly, he focused on more subtle forms of power than the economic. Instead, he was concerned with disciplinary forms of surveillance that seek to define, limit and contain human agency. In particular, his obsession with crime and deviance offers a final defiance to the borders that normative culture imposed upon a career that was so often divided between a very personal commitment to creative artistic self-fashioning and slavish subservience to public demand.

1
Little Lord Fauntleroy of the Valleys

One of Davies's most formative associations, and one that informed a great deal of his reception in the first half of his career, was with the working-class community of Blaenclydach where he lived from his birth in 1901 until he left to work in Cardiff at the age of 18. Davies was one of six children (three boys and three girls) who grew up in a home behind and above their parents' shop, the Royal Stores. As the children of shopkeepers in the Rhondda in the first two decades of the twentieth century, Davies and his siblings were rudely well fed in a Blaenclydach of riots, unemployment and strikes. Davies, therefore, was part of a community of working people, but was also at one remove from it. His family was able to afford a servant and a horse and trap and was 'stylishly well-off in comparison to nearly all the shop's customers' (Davies, 1997: 23). His father helped to found the local Chamber of Commerce, the Liberal Club and the local golf club, eventually becoming a Freemason and, following Rhys's example, a convert to Anglicanism (Callard, 1994: 59). His mother had been an uncertified schoolteacher. As Davies confessed in a letter to Gilbert Fabes, the rare-books manager of Foyles, he was born a degree above the 'arab class' and 'was taught to look down [his] nose' at the 'attractive life of the gutter' (RD to GF 18 February 1930 HRHRC).

However removed from his community by economic circumstances, Davies was nonetheless a part of that community. The shop was a meeting-place for many of the people of the village, and the affairs and lives of Blaenclydach were shared between the shop's customers. Indeed, the livelihood of the shop rested upon the same foundation as did the livelihoods of the miners who patronized it: coal. Despite this shared economic dependence, the shop owner does not often fare well within the English-language Welsh novel. Richard Llewellyn and Lewis Jones present two particularly dark portraits of them in *How Green Was My Valley* and *We Live*, where the shopkeepers are greedy and selfish parasites, totally unsympathetic to the plight of the miners. For instance, in Jones's *We Live*, Mr Evans Cardi is staunchly against the miners and solely for himself and the success of his shop. Jones's grim pronouncement upon Cardi is a vivid murder-suicide, in which the shopkeeper cuts his wife's throat and hangs himself. In Llewellyn's *How Green Was My Valley*, the shopkeeper is a thief who is exposed for stealing chickens, beaten and run out of town.

Davies, however, presents a different picture of his parents and their shop, a picture that illustrates Davies's ambivalent identifications. He points out that throughout all the riots of the valley, including the Tonypandy Riots, his father's shop was never ransacked, and he credits this good fortune to his father's generosity and willingness to extend credit in times of need. In his semi-autobiographical novel, *Tomorrow to Fresh Woods* (1941), the character standing in for Davies's father feels a connection to the miners: 'Little capitalist though he was now, Roderick couldn't feel himself distinct and separate from the men' (Davies, 1941: 27). Far from fearing the riotousness of the strikers, Roderick recognizes that his fortunes and theirs are held in common:

> 'We've got to stick to the miners, Roderick said. Serious for a moment, he stared out of the window in the grey autumn dusk. 'We can't live without them,' he reminded her, 'that's how it is. We got to take pot luck with them. It's no good me trying to be a lord.' (ibid.: 57)

Davies's subsequent narration reinforces this sympathy for the shop owner and his stake in, and connection to, the life of the working community:

> In a strike the tradesman was a bigger loser than either the miner or the mine-owner. The miners hung idle about the place, living on credit;

the owner was without profit but was not losing any of the coal in his pits. But the tradesman handed out his stock without a cash return, worked daily in his shop without a wage, and dipped into his bank-balance to pay his wholesalers, who in their remote towns saw no reason to exclude mining districts from the principles of trade. No wonder Hannah sighed, apprehending that the tradesman was the poor thwacked donkey of this commercial system. (ibid.: 57)

Hannah is the fictionalized version of Davies's mother, and her perception of the tradesman's shared lot with the miners, though pessimistic enough here, is, at times, much more idealistic. While sternly safeguarding the family finances (like a lower middle-class version of the Welsh Mam), she is nonetheless rhapsodic about the place of the shop in the community: 'She felt the shop was as needed as a chapel. When old customers came in with their little grubby books and asked for bread, how could she deny them? And a thin slice of ham could sooth a hungry man like a hymn' (ibid.: 145). Davies imagines a very harmonious relationship that almost dispels the shattering shop windows of rioting strikers.

1. Rhys Davies in the 1920s

Naturally, this sense of belonging is incomplete. If we continue to regard *Tomorrow to Fresh Woods* as analogous to at least Davies's *sense* of his place in his community, then Penry, the young writer reared in the second half of the novel, must figure as a Davies who was painfully aware of his state of resident exile. For instance, when Penry sneaks into the strike-time soup kitchen to have two dinners in one evening, he is caught and made to feel his difference from the other children:

> Suddenly one said: 'Hoy, you're not supposed to be here, you're not poor and on strike.'
> 'He's cheating,' glared others, their attention drawn at last. 'It's Penry Bowen from that shop.'
> 'We are poor,' Penry declared, belligerently.
> 'No, you're not.' They gazed at him as if he had an awful rash. 'After our soup and pudding he is.'
> He looked at them sullenly, hating their repudiation, and wanting to stay. (ibid.: 147)

Just as Penry is both repudiated and wants to stay, so Davies felt both part of and excluded from the working-class community of Blaenclydach. His own class position was a conflicted one, and, throughout his writing, he identifies with the culture of his youth, but is aware of the obstacles to that identification.

This class difference, further, operates within the interstices of other identifications, for Davies clearly remembers his childhood in Wales as a site of contested identities. In the earliest pages of his autobiography, his Welsh, Nonconformist and lower middle-class identities are as ill-fitting and claustrophobic as his flannel shirt and Eton collar:

> The Sabbath change of shirt, following my weekly bathe, was a horror mainly because the fresh garment, by some vindictive alchemy of its washing a day or two before, carried extra crisp fire in its fangs; by the middle of the week the sweat-impregnated garment would lose much of this punishment. But also there was the victory of authority over my howling protest ... The evil shirt slipped on by my mother's capable

hands, something almost as tormenting followed. A neck contraption of cold, rigidly-starched linen, five inches deep and called an Eton collar (as a member of the lower middle class, I never wore the celluloid kind, which required no laundering) clamped my neck in halter discipline. Suit, stockings and boots were of lesser consequence and left no memory, except for a Little Lord Fauntleroy embarrassment of brown velvet tunic with a lace collar. (Davies, 1997: 17)

Davies remembers his childhood as a place of religious and social repression. The 'rigid' and 'deep' restrictions of middle-class Nonconformist values kept him 'clamped' into place and held down by the 'accusing finger' of the preacher 'thundering of [Davies's] guilt' from the pulpit. Further complicating things, his 'Little Lord Fauntleroy embarrassment' suggests a feminized re-classing that further distances him from the working-class masculinity.

These feminized class associations and these oppressive feelings of guilt highlight the other obvious barrier to Davies's identification with the working-class community of his youth: his homosexuality. Many have identified the male-centred working-class context of much of Welsh history and culture. Some of this work comes from historians, such as Deirdre Beddoe, Angela John and others, who argue that the emphasis of Welsh history 'has been placed on celebrating the land of our fathers' (John, 1991: 1): 'The icons of the making of modern Wales are powerful and familiar: coal-mining and slate-quarrying dominate the images of work in south and north respectively whilst rugby and male-voice choirs have frequently been made synonymous with recreation' (ibid.). Wales's powerful labour tradition occluded women's work and lives, and Nonconformity reinforced domestic values that removed women from the formal economy and created a Wales that was working class and oppressively masculine.

As Davies recalls in *Print of a Hare's Foot*, the world of the mining valley was a 'heavily masculine' one (Davies, 1997: 59) that repelled him even as he tried to identify with it. For instance, returning home one evening, he recalls the alienating sight of a group of colliers: 'I felt full of bad nerves as I alighted at raining

Tonypandy with a group of half-envied, drunken, football-match colliers, who bawled exuberantly as the familiar black engine hissed under the ugly bridge. This place wearied me. The trap was here' (Davies, 1995: 94). This masculine culture of sports and work directly touches upon Davies's sense of belonging and self. He half-envies the masculine camaraderie, but feels trapped by it as well. The 'exuberant' male voices contrast with the familiar sense of sexual guilt apparent in the vile, snake-like train that 'hissed under the ugly bridge'. He wishes to belong, but not in the narrow definitions of gender offered by his immediate context.

In reminiscences such as these, Davies remembers a Wales in which sensuality and the body had no place, and where closely guarded masculinity governed the order of life. Davies's autobiography, correspondence and fiction consistently convey a strong sense of alienation from and entrapment within the rhythms of life and work in Blaenclydach. In an undated but early letter to his friend and patron, Charles Lahr, he tells Lahr that he has returned home 'complete with [his] usual depression upon entering Wales' and that he 'always feel[s] like [he's] coming to a jail from which

2. Street view near Davies's childhood home, c.1900.
St Thomas's Anglican Church is visible in the background.

[he] won't be able to escape' (RD to CL undated SL V36 iii). This claustrophobic depression is even more grave in Davies's portrayal of life in the bleak mining valleys as a kind of living death. R. L. Mégroz reports Davies as having always thought of his youth in the Rhondda as a Lazarus-like 'burial, with [himself] lying somnolent in a coffin, but visually aware of the life going on above [him], and content to wait until the time came for [him] to rise and be [himself]' (quoted in Mégroz, 1932: 1–2). Davies elsewhere likens the geographical formation of the Rhondda valley to a coffin and enjoys the coincidence that its first shallow pit was sunk by a Walter Coffin (Davies, 1937a: 67). Even the surrounding hills are described as 'coffin-coloured' (Davies, 1941: 56), by a Davies who felt that a more authentic self could not live and find expression in Blaenclydach.

Not surprisingly, death and its paraphernalia are important features in the landscape of Davies's Wales, and are often symbolic of the deep repression of Welsh Nonconformity. Davies's first novel, *The Withered Root* (1927), portrays its protagonist, the young and fatally tempted revivalist preacher, Reuben Daniels, losing his faith in the people he works to save. He regards their souls as 'dark and impenetrable as death' (Davies, 1927b: 169) and realizes that their religion is a death-worshipping repudiation of life:

> Ah, he had stayed too long amid the tombs of life, in this stale and arid churchyard of religion, his young and vital body occupied in the fanatical obsessions of a death worshipping people. There was something far greater in life than this miserable wailing before God, who suddenly appeared before him as an image of Death, an emaciated visage wasted into a skull. (ibid.: 235)

Likewise, in *Rings on her Fingers* (1930), Edith Stephens flees from her life-destroying valley for London, and her experience reflects Davies's views on his childhood home and his own motivations for escape:

> The Valley became terrible to her. Sunk between the iron hills, vile black and miserable, the stretches of dwellings broken by the dirt-spewing pits, the grim colliers and hopeless accepting women, the stony chapels

and common shops – the monotony, the fearful monotony of the unending weeks, ah, at times she felt her mind was turning into a slab of stone, her soul petrifying within her. But what could be done? Nothing. (Davies, 1930a: 15)

Like the 'coffin' that Davies inhabited, Edith feels her mind petrifying into her own tombstone.

Similarly, Davies's third novel, *Count Your Blessings* (1932), begins with a beautifully morbid description of the protagonist's fanatically puritanical parents:

> Her father, one of those stony primitive Christians whose grim memorials are the chapels of Wales, discerned the impulse of evil in every action of the flesh; the pleasure he himself had frequently taken therein was always followed by periods of fanatic penance, aided by his wife, who thought of her body as a great sow that had imprisoned her soul. God would free them one day from the slimy walls of flesh that held their pure souls: until then one's only desire was to battle in fury with the horrid pleasure that was enacted in the body. (Davies, 1932: 7)

Jane's parents repudiate the sensual world with the same ecstatic desire for death seen in *The Withered Root*. It is no coincidence, therefore, that when Jane's father reads to her from scripture, the text is the story of Lazarus, and in Jane's case, like Davies's, there is a strong sense of rising from beneath the death of Nonconformity:

> Wide-eyed and grave, Jane listened. She saw the dead rise and come forth from the tomb, a napkin about his face. *Lord, by this time he stinketh.* Flesh was terrible, a thing of decay and death . . . Yet, she did not want to believe it of her own body: and she thought of her thin white skin. Her bosom issued from her narrow waist, like a white hyacinth breaking from its sheath, her white legs, freed of her flannel petticoats, she liked to stretch and kick with a nervous joy. (ibid.: 8)

Jane's parents try to bury their daughter's sensuality beneath their Nonconformist shame, the shame that creates a culture of silence regarding all things sexual, where children are 'conceived in the silence of forbidden processes' (ibid.: 7).

It is not surprising that a gay man in a culture dominated by working-class masculinity and Nonconformist respectability had few outlets for coming to terms with his marginalized sexuality. Davies, therefore, negotiated a complex identity in a context that consistently tried to draw clear borders around the messy and intersecting identifications that made up the vibrant and diverse cultures of the early twentieth-century Rhondda. Davies needed to engage the liminality of Wales in order to find and articulate his gay self: he found and articulated this gay identity through art.

2
'A rainbow wash of the mind'

Uncovering what it was like to grow up gay in Blaenclydach in the first two decades of the twentieth century is difficult, for, as Davies clearly demonstrates, the dominant forms of life occluded homosexuality, and there is almost no tradition of articulating this experience. The valleys that Dai Smith describes at the beginning of this book are localities whose parameters are 'known by those who need to know them'. Unfortunately, this need for knowing identity in terms of place is problematic for gay people, whose parameters are largely defined by those who do not need to know the gay, lesbian, bisexual and transgendered experience. What do we do with those like Davies who needed to define the borders of a gay Wales? Growing up in the Rhondda, Davies is a particularly good example of the need to construct an identity in a context where the resources to do so were completely lacking. As Eve Kosofsky Sedgwick explains,

> gay people, who seldom grow up in gay families; who are exposed to their culture's, if not their parents', high ambient homophobia long before either they or those who care for them know that they are among those who most urgently need to define themselves against it; . . . have with difficulty and always belatedly to patch together from fragments a community, a usable heritage, a politics of survival or resistance. (Sedgwick, 1990: 81)

Davies's fictional and autobiographical reconstructions of his childhood reveal just such a patching-together of a usable identity from within the available forms of identity construction.

For the most part, Davies's *métier* when it comes to his homosexuality is silence. Barbara Prys-Williams's research into the drafts of Davies's autobiography reveals the layers of self-editing and even deceit characterizing Davies's production of his public self. This self-consciousness results in a 'very coded autobiographical utterance, at times in outright censorship as he constructs the sort of textual self that he is prepared to allow others to see' (Prys-Williams, 2001: 22). Entire episodes dealing with homosexual scenes and characters were deleted, along with phrases like 'frustrated queer' and even, 'Well I'm buggered' (ibid.: 36).

As Davies wrote in a 1958 piece for the 'Our Contributors' series in *Wales* magazine,

> The blankness of the page waiting for notes about myself is more dismaying than page 1 of a projected new book. Temptations for exhibitionism! So much to conceal, evade, touch-up! Stolid facts such as 'Born 1903 in Blaenclydach, Rhondda', where I lived for eighteen years, seem to be unnecessary. (Davies, 1958: 7)

In fact, after Davies has told us about himself in all of his autobiographical pieces, after he has presented himself in all of his personas, it is the 'blankness of the page' that confronts us most emphatically; for Davies was an able exhibitionist and performer of his public identity. Even the purportedly 'stolid fact' of his birth in 1903 is a 'touch-up', for, according to the school register of Porth County School, Davies was born in 1901 (Jones, 1991: 68). Davies, more comfortable, it seems, with his fictions, cannot provide an honest account of himself, and we must content ourselves with deciphering what silences and 'blanknesses' he offers.

And these silences and blanknesses offer a great deal. Looking back on his childhood from his late thirties, in *Tomorrow to Fresh Woods*, and from his late sixties in *Print of a Hare's Foot*, Davies stretches the constrictive boundaries of his youth through elaborating the role of art and literature in providing release from the more narrow definitions of 'Welshness'. In particular, he frequently deployed a somewhat anachronistic aesthete dandyism in order to realign the parameters, play along the boundaries and challenge the supposedly fixed 'interior territory' of his 'home'.

One obvious example of Davies's engagement with the liminality of the Welsh working-class masculinity of his childhood is the Gentleman Collier, whose purpose in both *Print of a Hare's Foot* and *Tomorrow to Fresh Woods* is to publicly disrupt mutually defining codes of nation, class and gender. In *Tomorrow to Fresh Woods*, he wears 'a brown velvet jacket and a kind of knickerbockers with coloured stockings and buckled shoes' (Davies, 1941: 19), and though he had tried to court several of the girls in town, 'they were fluttered by his dandy oddness [and] didn't feel comfortable with him in the streets' (ibid.: 19). Roderick, the father of the shop-owning family whose history the novel follows, declares that he would 'give a nice gold watch to any woman who'd walk as far as the post-office with the fop' (ibid.: 20). His 'dandy oddness' is a discomforting public thwarting of convention that sets him apart from other men and removes him from the concourse of heterosexual exchange. In *Print of a Hare's Foot*, his oppositional nature and threatening male difference is even more apparent, and his alien manners are violently contrasted to the dominant masculinity of the community:

> There was no other like him. His landlady said he owned nine pairs of shoes which he polished as no other shoes had ever been polished. He wore smart jackets of maroon or green velvet, fanciful neckwear, kid gloves and no hat or cap on his long, carefully arranged Botticelli hair. Mrs Bowen Smallbag, the midwife, declared him a credit to the place. He was judged to have come from either England or America, but there was no traceable accent in his melodious diction. Working on the coalface in Number 1 pit of the Cambrian, he preferred the unfavoured night-shifts. He always chose his own groceries, his landlady cooking for him.
>
> It was approaching eleven o'clock when another lodger-customer, a bantam man swollen with Saturday-night bombast, lurched into the shop. Several excrescences always on his inflamed face had caused him to be nicknamed Jenkins Warts. A thickset, two-rooted beetroot of a man, for a moment he eyed the debonair Gentleman Collier with a lurking

belligerence, suddenly gripped a fistful of his velvet jacket and gave him a push against the counter, behind which my mother stood.

'I'm as good a man as you are!' he bawled, and struck a fighting stance. (Davies, 1997: 73)

The Gentleman Collier's difference reflects threateningly on his challenger's sense of self. Jenkins attacks the Gentleman Collier (whose class transgression is implied in his name) in terms of status, but we are made aware that his difference is also a national one, despite the conspicuous lack of an accent. He has not simply taken on airs beyond the station of a collier, but has made a more fundamental move beyond the scope and ken of this Welsh working-class community. Underwriting these supposed differences in class and nation is a challenge to the stability of the gender and sexual constructions coterminous with a Welsh working-class identity.

The Gentleman Collier's 'dandy oddness' is part of Davies's deployment of well established discourses of art, class and gender. Davies's movement away from the work and life of the Rhondda and towards art and literature was a clear movement away from working-class (and lower middle-class) associations and toward leisure-class ones. Artistic aspirations were not necessarily dependent upon, or essential to, industrial life, and were, therefore, somehow beyond it. Alan Sinfield explains that creativity, art and culture have long been associated with, first, femininity and, later, homosexuality. The dandy emerged in the nineteenth century along gendered class lines when the wealthy leisure class came under attack by their middle-class detractors. The perceived idleness of the leisure class was feminized in comparison to the earnest, industrious and manly middle-class. The dandy was one form of leisure-class resistance to middle-class hegemony. The strategy was 'to repudiate manly, middle-class authority by displaying conspicuous idleness, moral skepticism, and effeminacy; in other words, to be a dandy' (Sinfield, 1994: 69).

The dandy's same-sex association emerged 'at the moment when the leisured, effeminate, aesthetic dandy was discovered in same-sex practices' (ibid.: 121), which were dramatically instantiated and publicly distributed through the trials of Oscar Wilde. By the time Davies adopted the image of the dandy, its leisure-class and sexual associations were well established and had firmly cohered in the symbolic significance of Wilde. The eighth chapter of his autobiography is entitled 'Spats and a Malacca Stick', after the dandified posture he began to adopt.

That Davies was aware of the dandy's meaning in British culture is only too clear when we encounter Edgar Roberts in *Rings on Her Fingers* (1930), a character who probably derives in part from one of Davies's London jobs in the early 1920s, when he worked as an assistant to a gentleman's outfitter, where he developed his dandified fashion tastes (Callard, 1994: 60). Indeed, J. Lawrence Mitchell suggests that Edgar is a 'cruel self caricature' (Mitchell, 2001: 102) of Davies's own sexual dressing. Like the Gentleman Collier, Edgar is marked by the extravagance of his clothing. In Edgar's case, his sexuality is inverted into a fetishization of women's clothing. He returns from school 'refined to the point of effeminacy' with 'gold-embroidered purple cushion-covers, *crêpe-de-chine* pyjamas, an incense burner, and general air of velvet-footed superiority' (Davies, 1930a: 49). From 'pince-nez' to 'spats', he 'was as elegant as a dolly' (ibid.) and had developed a lisp. Heir to a draper's shop, Edgar is enamoured of women's clothing. He longs for a woman

> who would know why he loved silks and colours, why he was thrown into ecstatic passion by cunningly woven brocades and women's gowns fragile and delicate as the music of Mozart, why a rich sunset reminded him of garlands of marvellously dyed crepe-de-chine hung in the sky, how he would worship her, this remarkable woman. (Davies, 1930a: 66–7)

Edgar is as removed from the realm of heterosexual desire as he is from masculine culture. He makes 'few men friends' (ibid.: 54), finding the male population of the valley 'coarse and lurid' (ibid.): the colliers are a 'heated and loosened ... thronging' mass (ibid.), and the middle-class section is composed of 'card-players, footballers, more drunkards and fools' (ibid.). Edgar laments that there

3. Rhys Davies, aged 20.

is 'no one with whom he could discuss the music of Debussy, the latest chic from Paris, the amorous palpitations of his soul' (ibid.). He relates to neither the rough working class nor the superficial middle class. His associations are aesthetic and elitist, and his manner is feminized, all in accordance with the established discourse of the modern queer.

Davies's personal uses of the dandy accord well with both *Print of a Hare's Foot* and *Tomorrow to Fresh Woods*, which depict the artist's trajectory out of their limiting mining valleys and into the life of cosmopolitan London. When Davies left Blaenclydach School for Porth County School at the age of 12, he discovered a passion for literature, which he nurtured after giving up all formal education at 14 to work in his father's shop. As he recalls, the meagre collection of books at home and the slightly more varied collection at the branch library of the South Wales Miners' Federation 'whisked the Rhondda world away' (Davies, 1997: 78). By 15, Davies had discovered a world of fiction that helped to form an identity in opposition to the dominant forms of life surrounding him. In *Tomorrow to Fresh Woods*, Penry makes the same escape. He tries to work in a local bank, but has 'a feeling of having left his real self leaning against the door-post outside, where it patiently awaited his return' (Davies, 1941a: 203). He 'had an obscure feeling of having been bamboozled into a dreary bondage he had not been aware of. He heard the clank of chains' (ibid.: 204). Like Davies's construction of himself in *Print of a Hare's Foot*, Penry's 'real self' is found in literature. For him, too, books become his 'truest solace' (ibid.: 227), and as he discovers 'the French novelists, Balzac, Zola and Flaubert, and the Russian Tolstoy, in translation in the local miners' library . . . Their air of the great world blew over him in great refreshing waves' (ibid.). Both Penry and Davies move through their communities and their narratives at an aesthetic remove, supplementing their industrial worlds with quotations of poetry and reminiscences of literary works.

Davies's use of art in *Print of a Hare's Foot* and *Tomorrow to Fresh Woods* is closely connected to his undisclosed sexual identity. For instance, in *Print of a Hare's Foot*, tucked exactly between a quotation from *The Duchess of Malfi* and his list of his favourite French authors, Davies makes some fairly ambiguous statements:

> The oyster shell of a boy's mind is forced open at random. Or he reaches to what he wants with a crab's oblique approach. I did not share my tastes with anyone; for street companions I preferred the simple boys who could even be called rough, and rarely discovered them to be rough. (Davies, 1997: 78)

One assumes that the 'tastes' that Davies does not share are his literary ones. This makes sense, given that his 'simple' and 'rough' companions presumably would not relate to his artistic difference. But we are left guessing what exactly Davies must reach for 'obliquely'. I suggest that Davies's literary tastes are an oblique reaching for an unstated sexual desire: that Davies is relying upon the well established association between the artistic, the feminine and the queer. The reference to 'tastes' moves ambiguously into both literature and rough boys, and the semi-colon between Davies's statement of his secret tastes and his choice of companions suggests a connection between the two. There is an association, therefore, between Davies's taste for literature and his taste for 'rough' companions whom he 'never found to be rough'.

These companions are more vividly figured in Penry's idolization of the miner, John, which is accompanied by Penry's drunken poetic incontinence as he quotes from Shakespeare's sonnets, Glendower's 'vasty deeps' speech in *1 Henry IV*, Keats's 'Ode to a Nightingale' and Thomas Campion's *Third Book of Airs* (Davies, 1941: 215–17). Penry's drunken poetic release culminates in a naked frolic in a pool. When Penry sees 'the hard sculptured flesh of the young miner', a 'flame [runs] through him like a terror'. He likens John to the biblical David and, when 'they [struggle] in a wild embrace . . . [coming] up chest to chest', Penry discovers 'the very secret of sensual savage joy': 'This was abandon', Penry feels, and he is 'jarred' to hear shame in John's voice when their naked rough-housing is at an end (ibid.: 218–20). In his relationship with John, Penry, the young artist with a taste for poetry, more vividly illustrates the ambiguous 'tastes' obliquely reached for in *Print of a Hare's Foot*.

Like Sinfield, Davies locates the fusion of artistic extravagance with sexual extravagance in the discursive power of Oscar Wilde. While neither Penry nor Davies includes Oscar Wilde in their lists of authors who offered them release from their Rhondda worlds, in 1946 Davies gave us reason to suspect the omission by including Wilde in an unpublished autobiographical piece that addresses the same literary escapes as *Tomorrow to Fresh Woods* and *Print of a Hare's Foot*:

> Had read very few books – there were few in the Rhondda – but at age of fifteen a volume of Zola (translated) came into my hands, the first 'modern' novel for me to read; it amazed me and startled me. Thereafter I conceived a passion for French literature and my earliest influence was Anatole France whose complete works – in translation – I eventually acquired. This was followed by Flaubert (who cleaned up in me, I think,

much of the meretricious element in A. France); *Madame Bovary* became for some years my Bible. I also read Balzac. But rarely an English novel, though Oscar Wilde fascinated me (probably because of the strong French influence in his work). This was all during my adolescence and was bound up in my instinctive urge to flee from the Rhondda Valley. (NLW MS 20897 E 1)

It is unlikely that Davies could have been unaware of Wilde's potent symbolic power as a signifier of homosexuality, yet he dismisses his 'fascination' with Wilde as purely academic. That Wilde is either a fictional addition here or an omission from the analogous moments in *Tomorrow to Fresh Woods* and *Print of a Hare's Foot*, strongly indicates that Davies made an active decision in the deployment of Wilde within his life-story. Whether Wilde is an omission or an addition, Davies is sensitive to Wilde's value as a signifier of both aesthetic difference and sexual transgression.

Wilde eventually does figure in Davies's recollections of his sexual coming-of-age. As Barbara Prys-Williams claims, Wilde operates as a kind of substitute vocabulary for a knowledge that Davies either did not have words for then or would not put words to when writing his autobiography years later (Prys-Williams, 2001: 110). When Davies was in his late teens, around the time that he wrote 'many dozens of Sapphics' and discovered 'heady Swinburne' (Davies, 1997: 95), an unsuccessful sexual encounter with a woman brought him to a sense of his sexual orientation, or at least of 'something decisive belonging entirely to [his] own identity, unrelated to this woman' (ibid.: 92). Shortly after this unfulfilling heterosexual experience, Davies found consolation in an edition of *Salome* with the Beardsley drawings. The drawings more than the play itself 'restored his nerves' (ibid.: 95). He tells us that he delighted in the '*perverse yet truthful* human beings' (ibid., italics added) that set off '[r]andom little bombs . . . inside [him] with *secret* detonations' (ibid., italics added). He read the book in bed and tells us that '[o]f course [he] consummated the revelation' (ibid.). The second draft of *Print of a Hare's Foot* shows that Davies chose the word 'consummated' over the original (and less subtle), 'masturbated' (NLW 21533 C 123), making the sexually liberating value of Beardsley's *Salome*, and the erotic significance Davies ascribes to art in general, all the more evident.

Taken together, the working-class masculinity, Nonconformist sexual repression and middle-class respectability had all exiled Davies from Wales long before he left for the creative possibilities of London. When he arrived in London, Davies's escape into art was repeated with gusto in his encounter with Diaghilev's Russian Ballet, when, in the early 1920s, he was finally liberated into the bohemian world of London as a young man:

> The curtain rose on an item entitled *Contes russes*. Its eruption of barbarically primary colours gave much more than visual impact; colour shot down the throat, attacked the spine, poked up an erotic tumult. The dancers leapt with extraordinary abandon or stood flower-still with classic grace. Best of all was the last item, the balls-shaking *Prince Igor*, its warriors dancing as only Russians can dance those Polovtsian exuberances. Diaghilev gave his ballets a signature and triumphant dash I was not to see equalled, their predominant sensuality achieving a purity which reached the androgynous. They were a Slav fusion of robust flesh become colour and running lines of poetry . . . After life in the Rhondda Valley the heap of ballets I saw was a rainbow wash of the mind. They assisted at liberation. (Davies, 1997: 109)

This is not simply an aesthetic wonder but a physical 'balls-shaking', 'erotic tumult' and 'fusion of robust flesh [and] . . . running lines of poetry' that finally and forever washed the Rhondda repressions from Davies's imagination.

3
A bohemian in Grub Street

When Davies began his career in London in the 1920s, his escape into Bohemia was not as simple as he might have hoped. Art might have been liberating in Davies's efforts to escape the Rhondda, but, when he began his literary career, he discovered that writing had its own set of economic restrictions. His movements throughout the late 1920s, 1930s and 1940s correspond to this tension between artistic bohemian freedom and frustrated economic captivity. In 1928 and 1929, funded by an advance on the American edition of *The Withered Root*, he spent six months in Nice, Bandol and Paris, and, in the winter of 1931, he travelled to Italy. However, despite these Continental excursions, and despite Davies's escape to London, he spent much of his time in Blaenclydach. On his return from France, he spent most of 1929 in his parents' home. Most of 1931 was also spent in Blaenclydach and, despite his discomfort in Wales, he consistently returned to his childhood home for months at a time, spending almost a full year there in 1941 while writing *Tomorrow to Fresh Woods*.

As a young man embarking on a career as a writer, this continued connection to his narrow Welsh origins troubled Davies. As he explained to Charles Lahr, his distance from his family was closely related to his literary ambitions. After his family visited him in London in 1928, he saw them off with a feeling of relief and an expression of defiance:

> They've all gone back to Wales at last. I was glad to see the retreating back of my sister. She is particularly irritating. The worst of it is, she's not like my other sister, who obviously has no use for me and thus

leaves me in peace – this one professes affection which she ferociously manifests as a sort of duty. Irritating!

But they are all filled with horror at my intention to abandon all jobs except writing. Platitudes have been trotted out with ruthless zeal. (RD to CL undated SL V36 iii)

This continued frustration with Wales and its restrictive influence reappears in an unpublished story called 'Interlude' (1929). This story is semi-autobiographical in its focus on a young writer returning from London to his home in a Welsh mining town. In this fictional retelling, the incompatibility of the mining family and the young artist mounts to a violent antipathy:

> He trembled on the verge of one of his outbursts now. Insult and abuse began to form in his mind, wrecking its former vision. Their faces poised about the dusky, crockery-littered table, were devilishly repellent to him. Yet he knew their hearts were really kindly disposed. But above all he hated them to allude to his book. The few things of his that were published had been so resolutely and grotesquely criticized by them, their uncouth conventions pawing them about, that he could not bear now to listen to the slightest mention of his writings. He set his lips, his heart throbbed, he looked before him dimly. What did it matter? He must just go away. Nothing mattered but his own intense flame of creation. (SL V 54 vii 6–7)

The 'flame of creation' burns in spite of his dull and insensitive surroundings, and the young writer is offended by the inability of his family to understand his work. This offence, further, has a basis in fact, for Davies's own mother refused to read anything he wrote after she had read 'The Sisters' (1926). In 'Interlude', Davies relates the experience of realizing that his family in Wales did not represent his readers. They were not the public for whom he wrote. Therefore, when Davies began his career writing *of* working-class Wales, he was not writing *for* working-class Wales.

4. William Roberts's Vorticist cover for the second number of
The New Coterie (Spring 1926).

Davies's earliest readers were the leftist highbrow readers of London. His first short stories appeared in a little magazine, edited by Russell Green, T. W. Earp and Paul Selver, called *The New Coterie*. Published by the German anarchist bookseller Charles Lahr, whose shop, The Progressive Bookshop, was also the magazine's headquarters, *The New Coterie* ran for six numbers, from November 1925 to autumn 1927, and included works by Liam O'Flaherty, T. F. Powys, Rupert Croft-Cooke, D. H. Lawrence, H. E. Bates, Aldous Huxley and many others. Davies's stories appeared in the spring, summer and autumn numbers of 1926. Initially attracted to the magazine by its 'strident William Roberts cover picture of threatening robots' (quoted in Mitchell, 1998: 80), Davies's stories about working-class south Wales were written in the dark, sordid and harshly critical tone of Caradoc Evans, and were accepted at once by Paul Selver. Following the publication of these stories, Davies became Lahr's cause célèbre. Lahr typed Davies's first novel, *The Withered Root*, and published Davies's *The Song of Songs and Other Stories* (1927), *Aaron* (1927) and *Tale* (1930).

Lahr and The Progressive Bookshop were the hub of a large literary and radical community that included, in the first instance, poets, novelists, critics, booksellers and publishers, and, in the second instance, leftist thinkers, activists and politicians of every shade between pink and red. This dusty, cluttered shop run by an eccentric German is the reason we know who Rhys Davies is today, for Lahr drew people from all walks of literary production, dissemination and reception, from writers to publishers to reviewers to booksellers to collectors. Lahr generously promoted countless young and aspiring artists, including Davies, while also assisting more established names. For instance, Lahr printed the first unexpurgated edition of D. H. Lawrence's *Pansies* (the manuscript of which Davies smuggled into England from France in 1929) and was offered the printing of the first authorized paperback edition of *Lady Chatterley's Lover* before it went to Edward Titus. As Kenneth Hopkins explains in his autobiography, *The Corruption of a Poet*, '[n]ot only did Charles know everybody, but everybody knew Charles, which is quite another thing' (Hopkins, 1954: 112). These words are another way of saying that even when Lahr was not directly involved in aiding specific individuals, he operated as a conduit through which writers, publishers, critics and booksellers communicated, through which connections were made and careers influenced. R. M. Fox remembers The Progressive Bookshop as a 'rendezvous for rebels and world shakers with an interest in books and ideas' (Fox, 1938: 180). Rupert Croft-Cooke describes it as a 'literary Rowton House' (Croft-Cooke, 1963: 130), to which 'most writers of the years between the wars, owe . . . a great debt' (ibid.: 131). Similarly, Hopkins jokes that the habitués of Lahr's shop were called customers only as a courtesy, for it really functioned more as a club (Hopkins, 1954: 108).

The life of The Progressive Bookshop was often a ragged Grub Street affair. Lahr himself was a notorious spendthrift, who sacrificed much of his meagre means to the young and hopeful artists around him. As a result, his shop catered to a bohemian crowd of artists whose virtue was the neglect they suffered. Rupert Croft-Cooke recalls that the Progressive Bookshop crowd,

> never expected, as writers or artists, to be anything but poor unless they hit the jackpot in their own profession. They were threadbare, ill-shod and unshaven, not in the abominably affected manner of today but because they had not the money to buy clothes and shoes, or, very often, razor blades. Naturally enough, success was unforgivable even to contributors of the *New Coterie* so that H. E. Bates was already looked upon with suspicion. Established writers were unmentionable except with contempt. (Croft-Cooke, 1963: 156–7)

Davies was just as much a victim of this paradox as any other habitué of The Progressive Bookshop: his first goal was professional esteem, but failing that, he would be a more legitimate artist *because* of his neglect by the established literary community.

This conflict between art and the market is central to the development of Davies's fictional themes, and is readily apparent in his correspondence throughout the 1930s (Osborne, 2008). In 1928, Davies wrote to Charles Lahr, 'I shall *have* to make my next novel more popular in theme. I mustn't get the reputation of being unsaleable' (RD to CL 1928 SL V 36 iii). Not long after, in 1932, he explained to Robert Gibbings, the chairman of the Golden Cockerel Press, 'I'm no Christmas author' (RD to RG 20 December 1932 HRHRC), and he complained to an American book-dealer in 1935, 'I don't suppose I ever will be a best seller!' (RD to HWS 3 July 1935 HRHRC). Again, in 1940, he wrote to his friend and fellow writer, George Bullock, 'But, alas, I'm beginning to see that it's not in me to write a best seller' (RD to GB July/Aug 1940 HRHRC).

At the same time, and in contrast to these self-conscious lamentations on his inability to sell, Davies made defensive affirmations of his purely 'literary' indifference to the market that excluded him. He claimed that his novel *Honey and Bread* had been a success 'at least from the literary point of view' (RD to HWS 3 July 1935 HRHRC). He wrote to a reviewer friend, G. H. West, that the cost and production of a special guinea edition of his story, 'The Skull', seems unnecessary 'from [their] "literary" point of view' (RD to GHW 13 July 1936, HRHRC). In 1942, he distinguished between the types of readers he ostensibly catered for in a letter to another friend and reviewer, Raymond Marriott: 'My book came out and appears to have pleased persons – literate persons, that is' (RD to RM 3 October 1932 NLW MS 20897 E). Finally, despite his dismissal of the 'unnecessary' special edition, in a 1931 essay on book collecting written for the rare-books manager of Foyles, Davies, who had three or four special editions behind him and the same number before him and no strong publisher in sight, wrote dismissively of mass market culture: 'In a world where the cinema, the two-penny lending library, tinned music and hysterical newspapers are becoming ever more popular, it is a relief to come across a leisurely designed book produced in the tradition, more or less, of the illuminated manuscripts of old' ('The Nose' HRHRC).

Essentially, however, in the 1920s and 1930s, Davies was eager to establish himself as a professional of some standing, and his first concern, as he explained in 1928 to poet and fellow *The New Coterie* contributor Philip Henderson, were the most basic ones:

> So you understand, don't you? The only thing to do, it seems to me, is to write a novel as quickly as possible and get an advance when completed. Publishers are interested in young writers. But not in poetry. They all cry novel. Chatto's, Gollancz, Capes, and Putnams have all written to me. But what's the good when I've got nothing to show them? Work, work – I've got to work. But it's like facing an unpleasant operation to think of sitting down before a pad of paper.
>
> All I can say is get a couple of decently written novels done and you'll soon get enough to buy yourself a couple of sausages for dinner for at least a year. (RD to PH 16 September 1928 NLW MS 22003E 31)

Such crass considerations seem unsuited to an author who has just published in a magazine whose cover and title suggest an indifference to mainstream culture, but making money and building a respectable literary reputation were very much on Davies's mind at this time.

The life of the starving artist in bohemian London was appealing, compared to life in Blaenclydach, but Davies quickly realized that art alone would not save him from the grim repression of south Wales; only *selling* art would ensure complete escape. Writing to Lahr from his parents' home in the late 1920s, and frustrated by his dealings with publishers, Davies again imagines his childhood home as a kind of living death:

> Heard nothing from Cape yet. What a time! I'm getting perfectly sick of this waiting. Too late now, in any case, to get one out this autumn. Blast all publishers and blast literature – I do wish I could go to sleep and wake up with them and it gone cleanly out of my consciousness.
>
> Nothing to relate – I'm rapidly being mummified here. (RD to CL undated SL V 36 iii 26)

Davies wrote this letter shortly after returning from a five-month trip to France, a trip, significantly, that was made possible by an advance on the sales of an American edition of *The Withered Root*. This commercial success and the geographical mobility that it enabled were especially transformational. As he explained to Lahr, the trip continued his growing sense of liberation. Before he left for

France, his letters suggested that even London had not completely removed his sense of repression: 'If I like France, I don't want to come back to England, I've always felt out of place here' (RD to CL undated SL V36 iii). When he arrived in France, he seemed to have found what he was looking for:

> the colours are so vivid, and there are lovely perfumes, and, above all, and air of indolence everywhere. I am seldom depressed now, one's troubles seem to become very thin under this blue sky, and there's not, somehow, that horrible sense of repression one feels in England. All this of course might be due to me not being a slave to any conventional work and hours. (RD to CL undated SL V36 iii)

This release from the 'repression one feels in England' was not only due to the perfumes, pretty colours and a writer's leisure; while in France, and as a result of Charles Lahr's influence, Davies was also befriended by D. H. Lawrence. Needless to say, to a young writer from industrial Wales trying to establish a reputation for himself from within highbrow literary London, the fame and controversy of Lawrence would have been profoundly affecting. Lawrence's influence on Davies's writing, as we shall see time and time again, cannot be overstated.

Davies's need for personal and artistic freedom is closely associated with the kind of geographical mobility he enjoyed during his five months in France. Between 1926 and 1940, during the first stage of Davies's career, when he lived the life of a bohemian artist and became recognizable as a writer of the Welsh working class, Davies never really settled anywhere. From 1926 to 1929, he lived in Manor Park, Essex. Between 1930 and 1936, he lived in Maitland Park, and during the 1940s he lived in Maida Vale. However, starting in 1930, Davies spent much of each year in a house near Henley-on-Thames with Vincent Wells, an older gay man and director of a city brewing firm. Between 1938 and 1946, Davies spent most of every spring and summer with Wells, enjoying, as he explained to Lahr, the seclusion:

I am completely isolated in this house. There's not even a bus to Henley 9 miles away. The place is hidden among trees in a fold of the hills and right away from the main road. But the house itself is beautiful and the countryside enchanting. (RD to CL 5 May 1932 SL V36 iii)

Davies visited Wells until the house burned down in February 1946 and Wells retired to New Zealand (Callard, 1994: 63). So Davies's time was consistently divided between London, Henley and Blaenclydach, and interrupted by occasional trips to France and Germany in the late 1920s and early 1930s, to Italy in 1931, and to the south of France, Paris, Marseille and Malta in 1937. The Second World War restricted his movements, but after the war he travelled to Lugano and Venice in 1947 and to Cannes in 1949.

Davies's unsettled life physically parallels his unsettled identity. He habitually crossed not only national borders, but social–symbolic ones as well, living along the borders of the public, the private, the urban, the rural and the industrial. He moved between, first, a barely rooted existence in the public diversity of London, with all of the sexual and social possibility this entailed; second, a private queer domesticity in the middle-class rural holiday precincts of Henley; and, third, the grim economic hardships of a Rhondda that was both home and yet not home. None of these places could entirely satisfy Davies, so he was always looking forward to the next move, longing for the country when in London, and dreaming of

5. Rhys Davies in Final Marina, Italy, February 1930.

Soho when tucked away in the country. Writing from London to Louis Quinain, a country policeman in Surrey whom Davies visited throughout the early 1940s, he described one of his Maida Vale flats with grim displeasure: 'My nose drips but the tap freezes. I've got a racking cough. Took this room in Maida Vale: it's not my cup of tea at all: the usual shabby furnished room. . . . I'm not in it a lot actually' (RD to LQ 3 February 1942 NLW MS 23106 E 24). On the other hand, writing from Henley to a friend in London, he writes that 'Today [he thinks] of the sun on Soho. One is never satisfied to be where one is' (RD to RM 12 April 1939 NLW MS 20897 E 34). Living on insufficient earnings, constantly pumping publishers for advances and struggling to pay his typists, Davies lived very precariously for rather a long time, and it was not impossible that a letter could reach him after having been to three addresses (RD to LQ 1944 NLW MS 23106 E 45). Fortunately, he owned 'little more than a small, but expensive, wardrobe and a few crates of books and papers' (Callard, 1994: 63), which made his frequent moves more manageable.

Davies's experience along commercial, aesthetic, geographic and social borders are not easy to resolve and, in fact, trying to resolve them would only obscure the natural contradictory complexity inherent in negotiating a literary career across already conflicted identifications. For example, in 1928, when Davies wrote to Lahr from France describing Charlie Ashleigh as too 'terribly commercial', he acknowledged that he was himself also 'a little tainted with that, having been reared and working in that atmosphere', but Ashleigh, Davies claimed, had 'carried it to a nauseating degree' (RD to CL 14 November 1928 SL V 36 iii). Davies drew some rather fine lines here. He was in France, far from the repressions of Wales and England, living on the proceeds of his first literary success and dismissing his own awareness of the market as somehow contingent upon the working-class context of his youth in Wales. From its beginnings, Davies's career was characterized by such complex negotiations of his aesthetic, economic, national and sexual identifications.

4
A 'professional Welshman'

Davies's first and most obvious market was in the English demand for Welsh fiction. By 1936, Glyn Roberts was able to write an article in the *Western Mail* titled, 'They interpret Wales – in English'. The article pointed out that the English reading audience was being confronted with several novels a year which dealt specifically with Welsh life 'in a manner that arrest[ed] their attention' (Roberts, 1936). Chief among these writers, Roberts claimed, was Rhys Davies, a 'pure artist' who '[u]nder the benevolent wing of Charles Evans [Heinemann] in London and the somewhat larger one of Mr. Nelson Doubleday in New York, . . . [was], or should [have been], exempt from the economic worries which never yet failed, sentimental legends notwithstanding, to hamper a writer' (ibid.). According to Roberts, Davies was the fortunate recipient of a timely interest in Welsh life: 'at this moment, Englishmen and Americans and their wives and their daughters are interested in Wales, in the detail and pattern of Welsh life, in its realities, not the honest romances of Allen Raine and Miss Nepean' (ibid.). Roberts encouraged the readers of the *Western Mail* to pick up their pens and join the fray: 'Have you ever felt the urge to write a novel about your friends and your town? Well, write it, write it – now is your time. You may be famous – you may, to be unsublime but not so ridiculous, either, you may make money' (ibid.). Davies, savvy market writer that he was, could have been no less aware of this opportunity than was Roberts.

Of course, not everyone agreed with Glyn Roberts's call. By 1946, for instance, Pennar Davies expressed quite a different sentiment in the *Welsh Nationalist*:

> It is common knowledge that now a Welshman writing in English – so long as he jeers at Nonconformity – stands to gain nothing by concealing his Welshness. On the contrary, to have been born in Wales, or even to be able to boast of a great-grandmother who had a partiality to Welsh rabbit (mispronounced 'rarebit'), is a commercial asset and a stepping-stone to fame in the English literary world. (Aberpennar, 1946: 8)

These 'professional Welshmen', as Pennar Davies called them (ibid.), posed a serious threat to the cause of Welsh nationhood, and Rhys Davies, 'lost on the ocean of English life' (ibid.), was among the worst of those who served up Wales to English tastes.

To what extent do Pennar Davies's criticisms apply to Davies, or to what extent did Davies exploit his Welshness? Davies certainly could not have been insensitive to the fact that he was very strongly recognized and touted as a 'Welshman'. As one reviewer writes,

> Even if Mr. Rhys Davies's name was not what it was, it would be obvious that 'Rings on Her Fingers' was written by a Welshman. Not only is his setting a Welsh mining town, but there is *throughout the writing* a Celtic imagery and violence, an insistence on the importance of physical passion, and, it must be said, an entire lack of humour and, sometimes, of reason. (review of Rings on Her Fingers: 642; italics added)

As a description of Welsh writing, this passage is not as exhaustive as this reviewer might like to think. As an example of Davies's reception, it is typical. His writing is often read as *intrinsically* Welsh and he as the native informant. Further, the reviewer's reference to the branding effect of Davies's name is particularly telling, for Davies began his career by changing his name from Vivian Rees Davies to the more identifiably Welsh Rhys Davies. From then on, his name appeared on the covers of his books reinforcing his publishers' jacket designs and blurbs. The dust-jacket flap of Davies's 'Britain in Pictures' book, *The Story of Wales* (1943), reads,

> As he tells the story he fills in the landscape, draws in the character and evokes the very essence of his country and his people for in his own

writing are apparent those qualities of sensibility, imagination, humour and vigour which are the inheritance of every true Welshman. (italics added)

Though these two descriptions of Davies's writing differ somewhat in their perception of the true Welsh spirit (one apparently finds the Welsh humorous, while the other does not), and in their relation to Davies (one at the level of reception and the other at the level of production), both imagine Davies and his writing as *intrinsically* Welsh.

Further, Davies was apparently quite willing to market himself in this way. He even allowed himself to be fashioned into the representative Welshman through such ventures as *The Story of Wales* and the 1937 travel guide *My Wales*, in which he describes the 'individual Welsh spirit, poetic, imaginative, musically rowdy, its vision seldom wandering anywhere beyond Offa's Dyke' (Davies, 1937a: 13). These words sound suspiciously like the language deployed in the advertisements for his work and in the reviews which state authoritatively that Davies's writing reveals that 'he has Welsh life and character in the marrow of his bones' ('Welsh Tales', 1942: 449).

6. Rhys Davies as the professional writer in 1926

That these productions of the Welsh Davies were intended for an English readership is unavoidably clear in the advertisements for the 'My Country' series, of which Davies's *My Wales* is a part. Of the four books advertised at the back of *My Wales* (*My Ireland*, *My Scotland*, *My England* and *My Wales*), *My England* stands out as the anomaly. The advertisement for *My Ireland*, after explaining that the author's (Lord Dunsany's) Irish ancestry goes back to the twelfth century, insists that the book provides 'the *complete* character of a people' (italics added). Similarly, A. G. Macdonell *'clearly portrays'* the 'character and genius of his own people' (italics added). And Davies himself provides a *'full* description of modern life in that miniature but picturesque and lively land' (italics added). When one reads the advertisement for *My England*, however, one wonders if perhaps Edward Shanks does not know his country quite as well as the other writers seem to, for he does not *clearly portray* a *complete* or *full* description of anything, but 'emphasizes that this work is his England. It is England as he sees it'. These advertisements are sensitive to a readership that would be critical of representations of the Self, but quite comfortable with a totalizing representation of the Other.

On reading *My Wales*, it is apparent that Davies is aware that he is writing for an English audience. The earliest pages begin by addressing the English gaze, in the form of London schoolchildren's essay assignments on Wales. The several short pieces display a stereotypical perception of Wales that Davies, presumably, is going to rectify in *My Wales*. However, the entire prelude of the book is not about Wales, but about the relationship between Wales and England. It sets up *My Wales* as an extended narrative act of tourism. He reassures his English readership by stating that Wales now lives in 'amicable harmony with [its] grand neighbour, England' (Davies, 1937a: 19), and he invites the visitor who is weary of English life and who 'wishes to see something of the land's original atmosphere' to 'go *down* to see the Welsh people' (ibid., italics added). *My Wales*, published by Jarrolds, clearly situated Wales in an English context. It emerged from English publishers and made homage to an English readership, even going so far as to end with a chapter entitled, 'Holiday Trip', which provides a 'short trip across part of the country' (ibid.: 229), hitting all the hot-spots, and including Davies's insider's slant on each of these places. We are even invited into Davies's intimate visit with a farming family locked in a 'northern fastness of mountains' (ibid.: 254), where one finds a 'very old race of people . . . uncorrupted' (ibid.: 256).

The commitments of *My Wales* are trumpeted most loudly in the final pages of the book when Davies addresses the now famous arson of an RAF aerodrome under construction in Caernarfonshire, just three months before the completion of the book. The three arsonists, Saunders Lewis, D. J. Williams and Lewis Valentine, were all founding members of Plaid Cymru. Saunders Lewis was also a scholar and poet committed to illuminating and writing the Welsh-language literature of Wales, who defiantly pronounced in 1939 that there could be no Anglo-Welsh literature, as the term was an oxymoron that did nothing to halt the 'cosmopolitan industrial machine' infecting Wales and the 'purity' of the Welsh language (Lewis, 1939: 9–10). Davies, who came to the end of his book not long after these fires of revolt had died down, and while the furore they created still smouldered, saw the arson as a sign of the dangers of the Welsh nationalists who operated in '[i]solation in the haughtiness of tribal consciousness' (Davies, 1937a: 283).

In contrast, Davies, the well travelled cosmopolitan queer artist, longed for a more international, or at least more European, perspective, and attributed the cause of this 'rabid Nationalism' (ibid.: 284) to '[t]oo much in-breeding, both physical and spiritual . . . [and t]oo great an identification with the same limited associations [which result] either in a sense of deadness or in a neurotic scream' (ibid.). Despite his appeal for a less nationalist perspective, even here, Davies is mired in the racialist discourse that informs so much of his writing, and what comes out most strongly is his belief that the future of Wales is yoked to the destiny of England: a belief which is equally apparent in his fatalistic pronouncements upon the Welsh language: 'I do not believe the Welsh language has a future' (ibid.: 227). And, even more dismissively: 'To me it is a lovely tongue to be cultivated in the same way as some people cultivate orchids, or keep Persian cats: a hobby yielding much private delight and sometimes a prize at an exhibition' (ibid.: 219).

Davies's commitment to an English readership is as clear as his dismissal of Welsh readers. His views on the Welsh language in *My Wales* are written in the context of his reflections on the poor state of Welsh literature and his general distaste for the Welsh readership, in both English and Welsh. According to Davies, the literary market in Wales is English: 'Go into any bookshop in Wales', he states, 'and you will be in England' (ibid.: 227). Wales cannot sustain a 'full-bodied literature' (ibid.: 211) because it cannot support 'full-time writers' (ibid.) like himself: 'Amateurs are not enough; they cannot offer sustained work. But it would be difficult for a professional writer to live on the royalties of books in Welsh' (ibid.). And, as he later states, 'the chances are that good and sustained work is more likely to come from a writer who devotes his whole time and mind to literary creation than from those harried by the cares of teaching, preaching and shopkeeping' (ibid.: 222). In other words, a literature needs strong supporting institutions, and those institutions are in London, publish in English, and have sustained several 'professional Welshmen' far more successfully than Wales could ever have done for itself.

Naturally, the reaction from Wales to Welsh writers in London was defensive. Predictably, Davies had little patience for the cries of traitor and turncoat aimed at the departing backs of writers who wrote books on Wales for an English readership:

> If . . . the author is one of those peculiar people with a liking for things that are best forgotten, then howls go up. Columns of correspondence appear as the novel gets read by the public: warm letters protest that Welsh people *do not* do this, that, and the other; do not speak this way *nor* that way; do not go to bed in their day shirts; are not immoral and drunkards; do not eat peas with a knife; this is not a *true* mirror of Welsh life, but a lot of perverted trash, etc. (ibid.: 209–10)

While *My Wales* was published in 1937, its views reflect Davies's early career. So accustomed was he to criticism from Wales that when *Count Your Blessings* failed to receive an unequivocally critical review from the *Western Mail*, Davies exclaimed that he had received 'a disappointingly broad-minded [review] . . . They've given up abusing me. They even admit there's two sides to a medal' (RD to CL 28 February 1932 SL V 36 iii 32). Even earlier, in 1931, Davies contributed an essay titled 'Writing About the Welsh' to John Gawsworth's *Ten Contemporaries*, which offers a useful introduction to reading his early fiction:

> it is not a pleasant job to write stories of Welsh people. Writing in English, one is published in London and one has to battle with the ancient recoil of the English from Welsh life. Across the border, in Wales, books – especially novels – are looked upon as frivolous unnecessary things that cost money to obtain, that frequently encourage sin and blasphemy and provoke indolence, that sometimes even dare to criticize Welsh life. (Davies, 1931: 41)

Davies locates himself in a double bind, but it becomes clear in the course of the essay that he writes for an English audience and speaking as the native informant, in spite of that 'ancient recoil'. After criticizing the English antipathy to Wales, he explains that 'the Welsh, these misunderstandings of their neighbours forgotten, have their charms' (ibid.: 42). Their 'miniature nationality' is 'bucolic and simple', and they are 'beautifully child-like' (ibid.), with the 'stupid crudity of a child' and a 'natural amusing greed' (ibid.: 43).

5
A 'natural amusing greed'

Davies's earliest fiction further reflects his need to distance himself from Blaenclydach and Wales through adopting a self-conscious English colonial gaze that regards the Welsh as a child-like, stupid, crude and greedy race, living a life of moral corruption amid a wasted industrial landscape. As one reads these stories more closely, one sees that Davies's anti-Welsh representations are equally based in a Lawrentian misogynistic dismissal of the middle-class, middle-brow identity that Davies regarded as typical of the Nonconformist cult of respectability.

Wherever one looks in Davies's early stories, one cannot escape the sense of oppressive squalor where houses are 'all joined together in a coating of dirty grey cement' (Davies, 1996c: 29), with 'a strip of barren earth' behind (ibid.) and 'angry, sullen [hills] . . . littered with pig-sties and chicken cots' before (ibid.). This barren disorder serves as a backdrop for the dismissive gaze of Davies's primarily English readership, as is evident in the early story 'History' (1926). It begins with two English sisters, Fannie, a long-time resident, and Elizabeth, a new arrival, looking down on the valley:

> They climbed the wide stony path on Bryn Hyfryd, the rest of the Valley stretching away beneath them, smoking and seared with pits and broken rows of dwellings. Elizabeth, imposing and majestic with her sombre veils floating in the breeze, looked at the sky, the grey hills hunched sullenly together, the monotonous houses and many chapels littered over the floor of the Valley, and sighed.
>
> 'There's peace here,' she said. 'It's beautiful after Euston. I've thought sometimes I'd like to settle here. If the people weren't so funny, it would be just the place for a nice quiet life. I suppose one could get into their ways? You're getting something like them, Fanny'.

> Slowly they climbed to one of the upper reaches of the Valley – a narrow creek shut in at its far end by a curved mountain that rose swiftly and nakedly to the clouds. There was one pit, and about it the village squatted, rows of cottages with a little main street and seven little chapels. A stream of filthy water wavered from the mine and fell and crawled to the thicker stream in the main Valley. Now and again people passed the sisters and stared at Elizabeth with the direct and examining stare of the Welsh people. (Davies, 1996c: 38)

Like the rest of Fannie's English relations, who find 'in examining the raw squalor of a Welsh mining village some perverse interest [Fannie] could never understand' (ibid.), Elizabeth adopts a patronizing colonial gaze. This Welsh village is a welcome diversion from Euston, and a land over which this 'imposing and majestic' English conqueror with a queen's name and a Cockney accent may rule. She literally looks down on its 'sullen' and 'monotonous' houses and its chapels, 'littered over the floor' like so much discarded rubbish, and the entire scene strongly recalls Davies's entrapment in and escape from the Valleys: the scene is 'shut in', the 'little' village 'squats' and the stream 'crawls'. The inhabitants, with their essentialized Welsh stare and 'funny ways', resemble Davies's dismissive description of Wales's 'miniature nationality' (Davies, 1931: 42). Only the 'naked' and 'swift' mountains can 'rise' out of the valley to the clouds.

Although Davies's representation of Elizabeth is a comic one, the Welsh (mostly female) villagers come off no better, and probably worse. Elizabeth arrives in the valley after the early death of her third husband, and, on discovering that there is no tripe shop in the village, decides to open one. When the locals gather around her new shop sign, they read 'Elizabeth Ellis Tripedresser,' and gawk foolishly at the strange word attached to the proprietor's name:

> 'There's a funny word! What means it?'
> 'An old foreign word it is'.
> 'There's a foolish woman – putting up a word nobody understands.'
> One bright little woman said suddenly:

'Well, well, a last name of course it is. A liking for fancy names the English have. Tacked it on she has to bring attention. There – Mrs. Tripedresser she wants to be called.'

The mystery wasn't solved until Mr. Prys-Evans, the minister, came along and was asked his opinion. He had been to college and knew English as good as Welsh.

'People, people,' he said, 'her trade it is. She is going to sell tripe.'

A little crowd had gathered round him respectfully. The bright little woman exclaimed:

'Tripe! Ignorant we are, Mr. Prys-Evans. Indeed now, what does the old word mean?' (Davies, 1996c: 41)

This scene illustrates the gap in knowledge between the English and the Welsh, but does so through the quaint infantilization of the Welsh people.

Once the Welsh villagers learn that tripe is made from 'the dirty old pipes of animals' (ibid.), their self-professed ignorance turns to disgust and scorn of strange English ways, and they gleefully boycott Elizabeth's shop. However, determined that this Welsh defiance can be 'conquered' (ibid.: 40), Elizabeth posts a notice in her shop window advertising a 'free supper' (ibid.: 43), 'food free' (ibid.), and a 'free dish' (ibid.), presumably to overcome the 'Welsh dislike [of] originality' (ibid.: 42), as Fannie calls it, with the Welsh 'natural amusing greed' (Davies, 1931: 43), as Davies calls it. The ploy works, and the villagers declare tripe a 'dish fit for the Queen' (Davies, 1996c: 45).

The story ends by making much of the double meaning of 'tripe', as both the literal food presented in the story and something grossly false and nonsensical:

> Thus an astute widow caused tripe to be eaten in the Valley. Later, one who held a high position in the local Council offered the rich Elizabeth marriage. He was accepted, but the shop remained under her management always. And day after day she could be seen there, bright and triumphant, plump, and almost Welsh. (ibid.)

History was made in the valley, but the story plays out the larger history of Wales and England, in which Wales has consistently been force-fed English culture and values, albeit in a transformed fashion. Indeed, if we play up the connection between Elizabeth, 'bright and triumphant, . . . almost Welsh', and her queenly namesake, Elizabeth I, we may look back to when the administrative hierarchy of Wales traded culture and language for a greater role in the burgeoning English Empire. But it is too simple to suggest that 'History' presents a straightforward anti-colonialist critique of the English dominance of Wales. On the contrary, Davies suggests that these comic, ignorant and greedy Welsh folk get the 'history' they deserve.

The conflict in 'History' is not merely a national one, but a gendered and class-based one as well. The primary conflicts are between Elizabeth and the women of the village, and, throughout the story, the men are pushed to the background or dead. Elizabeth's greatest antagonist is the butcher's wife, who holds a jeering court across the street from the tripe shop. This feminine conflict makes sense, in that Elizabeth offers new and alien foods that threaten the integrity of the Welsh home. But Elizabeth is not simply a threat to domestic integrity, for she is also a businesswoman who maintains her power, even after marrying her anonymous fourth husband. Therefore, her undermining of Welsh independence is finally figured through an inversion of traditional gender roles: a kind of national emasculation and a sanctification of petit-bourgeois distance from the 'funny' Welsh working-class community.

This gendered conflict is consistent with Davies's persistent preference for female protagonists, but it also relates to the strong dose of misogyny in his fiction, for his earliest anti-Welsh stories are based in what he presents as distinctly feminine hypocrisies. 'A Gift of Death' (1926) depicts a woman's selfish vanity after the death of her strict Nonconformist father. In this story, Maria spoils herself, while scrimping on her father's funeral in defiance of 'the peering women's faces' (Davies, 1996c: 21) and 'voices of women talking' (ibid.: 22). In the end, she marries not for love but for petty female competition: 'no love have I got for any man. Marry you I will so that respected I'll be. And there's a surprise it will be for those women' (ibid.: 23). Similarly, 'The Sisters' concerns two sisters deviously competing for the affections of their lodger, who, at the end of the story, flees the house of scheming female seduction and jumps on a train to the English Midlands.

'Mrs. Evans Number Six' (1926) and 'The Stars, the World and the Women' (1930) are particularly strong examples of Davies's anti-Welsh misogyny. These stories demonstrate the ways in which Davies's attack on the Wales he had recently fled was as bound up in gender and class as it was in nation and sexuality. In particular, Davies associates Welsh working-class Nonconformist respectability with a feminized commodity culture that superficially aspires to middle-class identity status. This gendering of class is a common trend in this tradition of class representation, and it offers another clear example of the influence of D. H. Lawrence. Davies took on wholesale Lawrence's idealist representation of the working classes as a virile working man opposed to lower middle-class domestic consumerist femininity.

In 'The Stars, the World and the Women' (1930), the bookish and soulful collier, Bryn Watts, is pushed by an ambitious and superficial wife into a middle-class life that eventually kills him. Davies tells us that it 'was the process of making [Bryn] a gentleman that finished him' (Davies, 1996c: 103). Forced into 'half a dozen stiff, glazed contraptions for fixing around the neck – collars with long fronts attached . . . new black and spotted bows, cuffs, silk handkerchiefs, flimsy socks . . . and spats' (ibid.: 104), and paraded through the homes of a respectable middle-class avenue, Bryn comes to the realization that he 'had been deceived by the ways of women, giving credit to the wisdom of their minds and seduced by the delicacies of their hands' (ibid.: 105). He dies at the end of the story, in a violent and rapturous revolt against his wife's ambitions.

Similarly, as her residential name suggests, Mrs Evans Number Six is a fatally house-proud woman who believes that her status is visibly displayed in that time-honoured symbol of lower middle-class respectability, the untouchable, almost sacred, front room or parlour. Her life is governed by a cult of acquisition, through which the women of the 'row' continually measure their respective statuses:

> Mr. and Mrs. D. T. Evans lived in Number 6. They had been married and lived in the Row twelve years. During those years Mrs. Evans had created for herself an enviable reputation. She was without children, possessed the best collection of teapots in the Row, had three clocks, and on Sunday wore a hat made of real fur. Her collection of teapots was famous; she had twenty-seven – eight more than old Mrs. Hughes, Number 10, had possessed. It had been a race between the two women to collect the largest number, and there had been much heart burning and acrimony over it. Mrs. Evans had said that Mrs. Hughes starved her family in order to buy teapots: Mrs. Hughes believed that Mrs. Evans denied her husband his rights so that she might escape the burden of expensive consequences. However, Mrs. Evans' collection got larger, and finally her rival gave up the race and died. (ibid.: 29)

In this instance, female respectability coheres in domestic pride, class status and womanhood, all of which are perversely displayed in the fickle competition between two women who challenge each other's roles as wife and mother, while trying to establish the symbolic capital that crystallizes the security of those roles. Within this feminized domestic space, the parlour is the archetypal space of social status and an especially charged site of class anxiety.

The principal conflict of the story arises when one of Mrs Evans's neighbours acquires a piano, prompting Mrs Evans to demand an organ from her husband. Through denials of food and flesh, and finally lowering herself into sickness, Mrs Evans gets her organ, and the story ends with a vision of the parlour as a shrine to Mrs Evans's status:

> That evening the curtains were drawn back from the front room windows, the lamp was kept burning, its light shining on the dark wood and the bright gilt of the organ. Peace and serenity reigned in the house, and Mrs. Evans sat before the fire in pleased conversation with Mrs. Jones, smiling and nodding her head happily.
> God was good. He always gave triumph to those who worshipped faithfully. And from the first she knew she was better than any other

woman in the Row. And what did it matter that neither she nor Dai could play the organ? It was there, in the house, and the only one in the Row. (ibid.: 36)

Mrs Evans is a representative of an undiscerning, acquisitive and ignorant mass that is consistently coded as female.

So, while Davies's exile from Wales had much to do with his dis-identification with working-class Welsh masculinity in the land of his fathers, his earliest stories are most uncompromisingly critical of middle-class Welsh femininity in the land of his mothers.

6
A curious friendliness among the men

Davies is critical of working-class masculinity when it excludes a broader range of desires, but, as his misogynistic representations illustrate, he is also sympathetic towards working-class masculinity when it resists a feminized middle-class respectability. The explanation for this apparent inconsistency is complex. It has a great deal to do with Davies's efforts to establish himself as a serious artist, a role which, in the first two decades of the twentieth century, was expressly coded as masculine in order to differentiate 'true art' from the increasing mass production of print and entertainment media, which elite culture coded as feminine. It also has a great deal to do with Davies's efforts to identify with Wales as a gay man, which involved an erotic reclaiming of working-class masculinity. This obviously Lawrentian stance is especially evident in Davies's fourth novel, *The Red Hills* (1932; American edition 1933a), which he began writing while living in Nice in 1928 at the time of visiting and corresponding with Lawrence at his home in nearby Bandol.

The Red Hills tells the story of a love affair between the self-exiled miner Iorwerth and the middle-class rebel Virginia. Iorwerth is a fiercely independent miner with an artistic temperament who ekes out a simple living selling the coal from a disused level in the mountains outside the town, while Virginia is the prodigal daughter of a respectable chapel-going and coal-mining family. The tension of the story is in Iorwerth and Virginia's passionate resistance to the repressive conventions of the Nonconformist community. Iorwerth, in particular exemplifies the virile working-class artistic man whose authenticity unmasks the frail and feminized hypocrisies of Nonconformist consumer culture.

Early in the novel, Iorwerth is established in opposition to the unthinking masses he comes to reject as mindless and degraded: 'Massed humanity – how hateful and repulsive it was! He had made the mistake of trying to love humanity, of trying to idealize a raw mass of protoplasmic stuff moving blindly over the deserts of time' (Davies, 1933a: 63). Iorwerth decides not to labour in the service of 'a dirtily massed humanity' (ibid.: 41), but seeks 'his own personal salvation deep in himself through love and awareness of beauty . . . and art, a sensuality of perception, delight in the visible world' (ibid.: 46). In opposition to the working class that he has abandoned, Iorwerth stands as the sensitive and intelligent labourer, entirely individual and free from the moral surveillance of the 'respectable' community:

> each tried to outdo his neighbour in worldly possessions – sideboards, pianos, tombstones on family graves and heavy gold watch-chains to wear with their Sunday suits and bowler hats. And they mistrusted Iorwerth for the spirit of liberation that was in him; his spear-like directness his untrammelled laughter, the poise that came from his sense of equality with all that was fine and courageous in life, his simple enjoyment of sensuality, his ability to drink without becoming a sot: all the clear burning of a natural flame in him. (ibid.: 57–8)

Iorwerth is the counterpoint to the superficial and acquisitive community. Further, his association with beauty and art is significant for Davies as well. The 'natural flame' that burns in Iorwerth is basically analogous to the 'intense flame of creation' burning in Alun in 'Interlude', and the 'flame' that '[runs] through [Penry] like a terror' (Davies, 1941: 218) in *Tomorrow to Fresh Woods*, when Penry observes the artistic miner, John naked on the bank of the ravine.

Davies's working class is in fact perfectly contiguous with the artistic Davies. Davies's class 'sympathies' work within largely conventional novelistic structures, and his working class resolves into a safe product of an individual, often creative or artistic, mind. All of these visionary invocations of working-class men recall or prefigure Tudor Morris of *A Time to Laugh*. Tudor, who identifies with the workers rather than with his own middle class, is not simply representative, as one reviewer claimed, of 'a problem which many are facing [in the 1930s]' (Edwards, 1937: 157); he is, rather, the vantage point from which a deeply personal narrative is told, closely associated with Davies's own artistic act:

> In quiet remote moments he wondered if he was using the valley as a painter takes a canvas when he is stirred by a landscape and repeats it, charged with the colours of his own temperament, on the cloth. This act of creation was being performed with his own soul for canvas. He was painting there the sacred lineaments of the place and the groups of its oppressed damaged people. And in some way the vision had to be displayed, if only from the back of a rickety brake: he had to bring it forth, else suffer a kind of death, a spiritual suffocation. (Davies, 1937b: 251)

A *Time to Laugh* is told from the singular and privileged voice of the middle-class observer. Tudor's personal conflict and journey are set against a background of strikes and riots, and his reflections sound more like the familiar voice of Davies the artist's need to create. The novel in fact occupies the discursive realm of individual artistic creation rather than the political motivation of a class.

An early dialogue in *A Time to Laugh*, for example, clearly carries the same resistance found in Iowerth's rejection of massed humanity:

> 'My fight,' said Tudor, slowly as if he hadn't heard the last observation, 'is inside myself, yours outside. But the goal seems to be the same – physical and spiritual ease.'
>
> 'There doesn't seem to be any use for you to come among us then,' Billy said, a little sullenly.
>
> Melville, who was leaning forward as if tensely, his shoulders contracted, gazing into the fire, said in his strange voice of pain:
>
> 'He comes among us because I suppose we've chucked away most of the fears and taboos of organised society. He feels a certain amount of freedom among us . . . Isn't that true, Tudor?' he asked, his voice dragging. 'We do mean something to you, don't we?'
>
> 'You're alive,' Tudor said. (ibid.: 20–1)

Davies is less concerned with what the working classes *are* than with what they *mean to him*. In this case, as in much of his oeuvre, their passionate resistance to the 'fears and taboos' underlying the superficial cult of respectability provides a 'certain amount of freedom' that he longed for, artistically and sexually.

The narrow world of respectability threatening Iorwerth and Virginia in *The Red Hills* is, once again, a primarily feminine one. When Virginia's father worries for his daughter's reputation, his concern is based in a female world of moral authority:

> Especially you, Virginia, that the women-folk are interested in. Do you think that they don't notice you as you tramp over the hills? And gossiping at the doors they are everlastingly. No doubt the women of Bryn Street saw you come home out of that dip where the man lives. (Davies, 1933a: 109).

Virginia's stepmother is the representative of this female surveillance. Like Mrs Evans Number Six, her status is symbolized by her 'shining living-room, where each object was cleanly and rigidly in place' (ibid.: 87). When particularly scandalized by Virginia's behaviour, she 'swept in harsh dignity out to the parlour, where she lit the gas and occupied herself in moving the china bric-a-brac about, changing their places. The house was her pride and everything shone with the bright purity of Heaven itself' (ibid.: 104). Inevitably, Naomi is pushed aside in the novel's development of its themes. She falls to a stroke, caused, Davies informs us, by her own violently righteous hatred, and she dies.

Time and again, in Davies's fiction of the 1920s and 1930s, the uncritical, superficial and 'respectable' woman must be removed. Naomi dies to make room for the passionate young Iorwerth. Dr Tudor Morris of *A Time to Laugh* replaces a solicitor's daughter, Mildred, who 'would be the perfect wife, her house . . . [having] an ordered peace' (Davies, 1937b: 68), with the working-class Daisy, who 'behaved with a familiar confidence among the men' (ibid.: 11), and who had 'no sexual limitations, no coyness or conceit, no virtuous locking-up of her treasures' (ibid.: 27). Similarly, in

Jubilee Blues, the pit manager's daughter, Annie Vaughn, cannot descend to the poverty of her communist schoolteacher lover, David Morris. David dismisses her as a 'menial to money, to social position, to clothes even' (Davies, 1938: 172). She is eventually shunted off into a loveless 'bourgeois' marriage, having lost her chance of getting close to the 'true vital commonness' (ibid.: 61) of the novel's heroine, Cassie Jones, proprietress of the masculine world of the pub. David eventually turns his affections to his fellow communist, Violet Gwynne, with whom he goes on 'comradely hike[s]' (ibid.: 253), and whom Annie dismisses as 'boyish' (ibid.: 265) and 'not feminine enough for [David]' (ibid.), with her 'short hair, and flat body, and feet in thick brogues' (ibid.). Each of these menial, passionless, bourgeois women is a condemnation of a consuming mass culture of twin beds, tinned food and unplayed organs.

These superficial middle-class women are obstructions to a masculine working-class authenticity. For example, in *Rings on Her Fingers* (1930), when Edith Roberts is unsatisfied with her effeminate middle-class husband, Edgar, she contrasts him to the virile young miner, Hugh Richards. Edith wants desperately to 'create a *manliness* in' Edgar (Davies, 1930a: 131), and longs rhapsodically for the untainted striking miners:

> What a fine body of men they are! They're something pagan, as though they've preserved something of the original status of man, arisen out of the earth and achieving his living in direct contact with it. Rid the thing of all its disgusting commercial and industrial aspects and this Strike means the men are trying to protect their natural possessions from a stealthy and powerful ogre, a robber. (Davies, 1930a : 151)

This vital, pagan and highly aestheticized working-class masculinity is, of course, deeply implicated in Davies's gay difference, which was always at odds with the oppressive working-class masculinities of the industrial world he was often called upon to represent.

In *The Red Hills* and elsewhere, Davies translates the working world of men that has always excluded him into a homosocial world of same-sex compassion that reconciles his gayness with working-class masculinity. As Eve Kosofsky Sedgwick argues in *Between Men*, homosociality exists in an unbroken continuum with homosexuality (Sedgwick, 1985: 1), and part of homophobia's cultural power comes from the 'similarities between the most sanctioned forms of male-homosocial bonding, and the most reprobated expressions of male homosexual sociality. . . . For a man to be a man's man is separated only by an invisible, carefully blurred, always-already-crossed line from being "interested in men"' (ibid.: 89). Davies was fascinated with the homosociality of the miners, which he described in *Tomorrow to Fresh Woods* as an 'alien world with its atmosphere of the underground which [the miners] carried about with them, a sexless world of men' (Davies, 1941: 186). It is even more evident in *Jubilee Blues* (1938), where 'No hint of sex besmirched the austerity of these male Welsh pubs' (Davies, 1938: 42). In a scene that predicts the divestment and redressing of sexual identity found in 'Nightgown' (1942), discussed by Katie Gramich (2001), a cross-dressing woman secretly invades the homosocial purity of the pub, and the violation is met with horror and swift repair:

> Everybody wondered who the handsome young stranger was and, thinking he was a visitor from London or America, the regulars bought him drinks and encouraged him to tell his story. But with the sixth or seventh pint the stranger seemed to forget he was in a clean land, and his true nature began to come out. He ogled the men and tried to caress a big labourer, father of eleven children, who dropped his glass with a howl of fright and ran home. The regulars, after consultation, closed round the stranger and truculently demanded what he thought he was at. He was pushed about, though he only laughed lewdly. Finally, someone snatched off his hat, and long ropes of hair streamed down. The anger of the habitués increased to fury. She was bodily chucked out, with loud cries of abhorrence. The licensee used to declare that his trade went down for some time after this contamination: he certainly had the rooms ostentatiously spring-cleaned and redecorated. (Davies, 1938: 41–2)

On the surface, this scene suggests a simple gender conflict, but Davies makes much more of it. His use of the masculine pronoun to refer to the woman linguistically transforms her into the man that the pub's habitués *essentially* perceive her to be; when Davies writes of the ambiguous stranger's desire as '*his* true nature', he blurs the categories of gender identification and thereby introduces the threat of homosexuality into this homosocial world. The men become even more horrified to discover that the stranger is a woman, because the ease with which gender identity is performed challenges the stability of all gender identity. Defensively, therefore, the men 'consult' and 'close round' to re-establish a common masculinity, but the contamination is removed only after 'ostentatious redecoration', for all identity is by nature ostentatious and excessive.

While Davies is clearly aware of the exclusiveness of the homosocial world of work and the policing of gender that accompanies it, his particular depiction of those homosocial bonds is mingled with his queer expressiveness, or gaze, and he clearly exploits the close male bonds that threaten the inviolability of masculine culture. In a particularly vivid scene from *The Red Hills*, Davies illustrates an intimate and subterranean masculinity, in which Iorwerth enjoys a sensual, erotic and exotic scene of working men from his 'secret watching place' (Davies, 1933a: 29):

> Then sometimes, as he trudged about the galleries on some errand, he would pause to admire a gaunt beauty in a scene before him . . . perhaps a trio of men intent on their job on the face of the coal, the faint golden light of their three lamps shining on their naked, muscle-gripped torsos as they smashed at the coal between the slanted columns of timber that held the roof. Soon their white flesh would be black as a negro's; and then streams of sweat would stripe them like tigers. He would smile at them from his secret watching place, the three heaving men etched in a luminous circle amid enshrouding darkness. Somehow it was good to see them and witness their determination to wrest treasure a mile under the earth's crust. (ibid.)

M. Wynn Thomas regards Davies's frequent adoption of a sensual gaze located in 'the beautiful desirability of the male body' as an 'agonized' desire that finds oblique expression in much of Davies's fiction (Thomas, 1997: 4). This is certainly the case, but as this passage from *The Red Hills* continues, Davies goes further to reveal the strange contradictory compatibility of male-bonding (taken to the sexually threatening extreme in Iorwerth's sensual gaze) with the 'snarling' masculinity of the public world of daylight:

> And there was a curious friendliness among the men once they had descended the mine, an understanding that quietly eased the nerves, an unspoken bondage of protection towards each other which was beyond sentiment and peculiarly satisfying. It was only above that the snarling was expressed. 'Down-under', the world was knit in comradeship. (Davies, 1933a: 29)

Here, as elsewhere in Davies's fiction, the desire implied in Iorwerth's gaze is excluded by the policing of gender. This intense male bonding, this 'peculiarly satisfying' 'curious friendliness' must remain 'sexless', and, in the public light of day, masculinity must be 'snarlingly' reasserted and deviation policed. Nevertheless, the 'secret' desire has been unearthed and Welsh working-class masculinity realigned to accommodate Davies's queerness. Compare, for instance, Davies's later recollection of being 'full of bad nerves as [he] alighted at raining Tonypandy with a group of half-envied, drunken, football-match colliers' (Davies, 1997: 94), with this earlier effort to discover 'an understanding that quietly eased the nerves, an unspoken bondage of protection' with a need to be 'knit in comradeship'.

7
'The raw stuff of life'

Although Davies's thematic interests leaned far more toward passion than politics, and although he tended to present a colonialist infantilization and feminization of Wales, he was often circulated and received as a defender of Wales. This image was largely due to the fact that he began writing about the working classes in 1926, the year of the General Strike, and continued throughout the 1930s. As Stephen Knight points out, *The Withered Root* (1927), *Rings on Her Fingers* (1930), *Count Your Blessings* (1932) and the Glan Ystrad trilogy, *Honey and Bread* (1935), *A Time to Laugh* (1937) and *Jubilee Blues* (1938), had all been published by 1938. To put this in context, 'Davies had produced three industrial novels before Jack Jones had published one, and produced six before Lewis Jones had published his second' (Knight, 2001: 57). It can be argued that, in the 1930s, Davies was the foremost writer of the Welsh industrial experience. He was the first in what would soon amount to a more or less stable body of writers interpreting this new Welsh experience in the pages of novels.

When Davies wrote of south Wales mining communities, the literary market expected him to provide not only the authenticity of the Welsh insider, but the authenticity of the working-class insider as well. In fact, one authenticity depended upon the other. As far as many of his reviewers were concerned, Davies was a Rhondda boy and that was that. He had been raised for riots and had coal-dust in his veins. But, as a shop owner's son who had only been down in the mines once, and even then as an observer rather than a worker, there were limits to that authenticity. Of course, many other south Wales novelists were not workers. Glyn Jones and Gwyn Thomas were teachers, and Gwyn Jones was a university professor, but all of these men grew up in working-class families. Both Lewis Jones and Jack Jones were working men before they became involved in politics and eventually became writers. Only B. L. Coombes remained a miner following the success of his first novel, *These Poor Hands* (1939), and, from this position, he preached the doctrine of working-class authenticity loudly. In a BBC broadcast in 1947, his words read almost as a criticism of the expatriate Davies:

> If you, a working-class writer, leave the valleys and live for one year away from them . . . their lives and their thoughts will fade from among your closest memories, and in that interval many fresh problems will have arisen, which you know nothing about. Many a working-class writer has been ruined by going away from the only life he knows anything about, and trying to live on his mental capital. You won't catch me leaving my valley. (quoted in Jones and Williams, 1999: 61)

Coombes defends exactly that insider authenticity that many saw as the working-class writer's only true claim to publication.

The label of 'working-class writer' was not an easy fit for Davies, not only because of his lower middle-class origins, but because of his deeply personal identification as an artist. Unfortunately, a working-class writer's commitment to art was often regarded as suspect and, if not secondary to political action, then totally at odds with it, and perhaps even tainted with establishment privilege. For instance, listen to the language of this tribute to Lewis Jones, who was, incidentally, another Blaenclydach native and a contemporary of Davies, written shortly after Jones's death in 1939. Jones, it is contended, was not an artist but an activist, whose 'writing was only one of many modes of political activity simultaneously exercised' (Garman, 1935: 264). He 'was concerned much less with self-expression than with creating in his readers the will to act' (ibid.). His novels were 'firmly rooted in the life of a community' and were 'necessarily social to the extent that everyone's life is affected by, and almost all are dominated by, the pit' (ibid.: 265). Lewis Jones's *Cwmardy* (1937) and *We Live* (1939) are among the most clearly proletarian novels of the 1930s. Next to him, Davies is far from being a working-class author. Yet, largely due to his Welsh subject, Davies is frequently lumped in with Jones in the same category and spoken of in the same terms. Davies's fiction was regarded as having 'an attitude of greater humanity, and . . . a realisation that the common problems of mankind, taken in the mass, are not sexual, but simply economic' (Davies, 1940a: back flap of *Under the Rose*). Or, it 'exhibits a loose pattern of history as determined by the economic factor' and, with a 'naturalness of style', describes the life of a community

> which draws its livelihood from the . . . colliery . . ., of lavish feeding in days of prosperity, of faggots-and-peas nights in harder times, of Saturday nights in the pub and the demand for tinned peaches, of football, chapel, strikes and Socialism, the imaginative emphasis is on the fortunes of the coal industry and upon the money value of our civilization generally. ('Hard Times', 1941: 529)

This review praises a democratic and demotic writer who is sensitive to the economic base of social life. The reviewer's list demonstrates his pleasure with the documentary sweep he perceives in *Tomorrow to Fresh Woods*. And, in the review as a whole, one does not get the sense of a plot so much as of a place and its people, both of which, we are assured, Davies is more than qualified to present to his readers.

Davies's most fully realized treatment of the industrial experience of Wales is the Glan Ystrad trilogy of *Honey and Bread* (1935), *A Time to Laugh* (1937) and *Jubilee Blues* (1938), which maps the history of a south Wales valley from the sinking of the first pits in a fading idyll of mid nineteenth-century pastoralism to the fatal years of urban decay in the Depression. As Michael J. Dixon has convincingly demonstrated, these novels are not the realist proletarian novels they have often been received as, but are, in fact, deeply romantic in theme. As Dixon explains, 'in writing these "industrial" novels Davies was opportunistically adapting to the fashion for proletarian literature prevalent amongst the English "liberal" middle classes of the 1930s, who made up much of his readership' (Dixon, 2001: 40).

Dixon's claims are confirmed by the trilogy's origins in Davies's correspondence with one of the representatives of that 'liberal' English readership. The Glan Ystrad trilogy partly came into being through Davies's long dialogue with G. H. West, a reviewer for *The Times Literary Supplement*, a periodical that Davies trusted implicitly. West reviewed much of Davies's writing and read a number of his novels in manuscript, including the Glan Ystrad trilogy, and in his correspondence with West, Davies constantly struggled with the appropriateness of his modes of representation to his working-class themes. West and Davies debated the latter's writing over a period of six years, moving along the boundaries of politics, art and the market.

In his letters to West, Davies expresses a political commitment and reveals his movement toward a narrative of sociological significance; however, these letters also express his conflict with that goal, realizing that his preferred modes of expression tended towards the individual rather than the social, and towards the personal and passionate rather than the political and revolutionary. For instance, when West criticized *The Red Hills* for turning 'rather too readily to his hero and heroine as seen in isolation, in hillside detachment, from their environment' (West, 1932: 960), Davies wrote back to complain of West's designs upon his writing:

> I see you are still pining for me to produce a thousand page novel, complete with every damned detail down to the lump of soap in the kitchen and the pattern of the linoleum under the beds. Can't you see that my characters' environment is intrinsic in their behaviour, their conversation, their thoughts, in a given situation and set of circumstances such as in the 'Red Hills'? I can't help it if the Times and publishers call it a novel and charge 7/6 for it. Fiction seems to me a matter of concentration, and the more successfully it's done (in degree of concentration, I mean) the better the artist. I'd rather pay 7/6 for

the 30 pages of Maupassant's 'Miss Harriet' or Tchekhov's 'The Bishop' than for the 'Old Wives' Tale' or 'Anna Karenina' . . . Of course I don't see myself on a level with these people, but the above are my aims and beliefs. I never felt myself bowing and prostrate before size and bulk: in fact I've always been suspicious as to the imaginative capability of its producer. (RD to GHW 25 November 1932 HRHRC)

West apparently wanted a naturalist style, and this desire is largely the result of Davies's Welsh working-class subject, which Davies referred to in another letter to West as 'the growls and barking people seem to expect of [him] as a Welsh novelist' (RD to GHW 3 May 1935 HRHRC). Davies, however, obviously resisted West, claiming the artist's autonomy, and privileging the short story as the more artistic medium, by virtue of its unmarketability and its tendency toward lyricism, rather than reportage. He resists West as part of an apparatus that has designs upon what sort of novel he should write.

By the end of his correspondence with West, nearly six years and several exchanges later, Davies had quite a different vision of his writing. He had completed the trilogy (1,107 pages in all), and wrote of it in the social and historical terms that West demanded. Of the third novel in the series, *Jubilee Blues*, he explained to West,

> I realize the slowness of the first 100 or so pages – due, I think, to the swerving away from the personal development of Cassie and Prosser as a married couple to mere 'reporting' of the General Strike and its effects on a community, and the other happenings that do not arise from the actions of one's characters. It's terribly difficult to incorporate social matters and mass affairs into an imaginative work; and the intrusion of fact seems to deaden one's faculties. However, no doubt there is a way of achieving this blend successfully – undiscovered by me, as yet. (RD to GHW 31 August 1938 HRHRC)

These two letters represent only a brief sampling of Davies's interaction with his reviewer, but they clearly illustrate the pressures influencing this author to write something quite different from the novels to which he was accustomed. Davies tried to conceive of a story in a manner unfamiliar to him, but supposedly called for by the times, or least by *The Times*.

The trilogy succeeded in living up to expectations. The reviewers found a writer who was deeply committed to the cause of labour and who wrote with the authentic, spare, unadorned voice of the worker rather than the 'artifice' of the artist. When V. S. Pritchett referred to *A Time to Laugh* among five novels reviewed under the title 'Political Novels', he described one author as 'deeply, gravely committed' (ibid.), and Davies himself as 'out in the streets when the windows smash' (Pritchett, 1937: 428). The *TLS* review of *Jubilee Blues* takes a similar tack, extolling Davies's commitment to the history he describes and his knowledge of the living voice of the people:

> Every type and circumstance come into the picture – the talkers and the silent, the man on short-time who reads Spinoza, the boy taken away from grammar school to replace his father in the pit, the half-bankrupt tradespeople, the grim or grizzling women. There is a doctor who has thrown in his lot with the colliers; there is the restless fury of his schoolmaster son, thwarted in love by a code of gentility he despises. ('Woman of Wales', 1938: 659)

As *Jubilee Blues* focuses on the proprietors of a pub, the principal setting allows for the life of a community to pass through the narrative, and this reviewer is keenly aware of this novel's depiction of the living, working community and its ability to confront the reader with 'problems that the conscience cannot ignore' (ibid.). In keeping with his representation of the people, Davies's writing is regarded as imbued with the same honest simplicity of an idealized working-class voice:

> It is not altogether a polished piece of work – Mr. Davies has almost too swift and flowing an imagination for that – and here and there his gusto gets the better of his judgement. But it has a liveliness and humanity such as few of our younger novelists exhibit and without which all the literary polish in the world is of small account. (ibid.)

The authenticity of Davies's writing is partly due to his lack of 'polish', which would only interfere, presumably, with the 'humanity' he represents.

Despite Davies's efforts to write to the expectations of reviewers and readerships, his stories and novels dealing with the Welsh working class were not entirely market driven. While he was insecure about being identified as a working-class writer, one must acknowledge his unmistakable sympathies with the conditions of working life. In an early feature on Davies in the *Western Mail*, he characterized himself as a sympathetic advocate of the working classes:

> I have been brought to task for my apparent 'cruelty' to the working classes, but that is the last thing I would wish to be, for my sympathy with the Welsh proletariat is very real and very deep. I do feel, however, that there are in Wales phases of life and types of humanity so raw and crude that if one writes of them with sincerity, one might easily appear to be cruel. (Davies, 1927a)

Davies suggests that the 'rawness' of life in Wales transcends any intent he may have had as a writer, that his craft is secondary to and determined by his subject. It would seem that such a 'raw' and true existence is opposed to over-cultivated notions of art and culture. This contrast persists well into Davies's career. While writing *Tomorrow to Fresh Woods* (1941), Davies returned to Blaenclydach, as he claimed that 'living [there was] a great aid to collecting material' for the novel (RD to LQ 18 Jan. 1941 NLW MS 23106 E 7). While there, he wrote to Raymond Marriott describing his return to Blaenclydach and his representation of its working community as his access to that same 'raw' authenticity:

> About six or seven years ago I turned my back on the 'artistic' crowd in fear – not that some virtue or vitality is entirely absent from them, but because their world is too enclosed and parasitic. One wants to get back to the raw stuff of life. It is down here, though even here it's more impure than it used to be. (Or is this because, corrupted, I cannot detect it so keenly now?). By 'raw stuff of life' I mean the original simplicity

in man, that primal glow in him which gives him meaning in a blind world. (RD to RM First Sunday After Easter 1941 NLW MS 20897 52)

Echoing Davies's letter to Marriott, the Penry who in *Tomorrow to Fresh Woods* leaves for London to become a writer is also the Penry who, like Davies, looks upon the working community of his home town as proud and noble: 'These dark rigid rows of stone houses, they too contained richnesses. Here too life spilled its wild purple. In these squalid houses were dealings with *the raw stuff of life*, here were the eternal hungers' (Davies, 1941: 194). Here, presumably, where the 'eternal hungers' bring one closer to true living, one escapes such artificial worlds as those of artistic bohemian pretension.

Indeed, much of Davies's sympathy for the working classes was indeed 'very real and very deep', particularly during the Depression and the years leading up to and including the Second World War. Stories like 'The Two Friends' (1936), 'On the Tip' (1936), 'The Pits are on the Top' (1942) and 'Nightgown' (1942) express an intimate understanding of the effects of economic injustice on individuals, families and communities.

'On the Tip' is a particularly affecting story that couples an indictment of the dehumanizing conditions of the south Wales valleys in the 1930s with a progressive political sentiment of defiant human perseverance. In this story, the tip symbolizes the dark, dirty, precarious and insecure nature of the coal industry, which is the ugly reality behind the relatively brief period of prosperity:

> The 'tip', as it is called, fringes the colliery like a cliff, falling away precipitately from the plateau on the hillside where the shafts of the pit rise. It is a gigantic cape of black, stony waste stuff, the rubble unearthed with the coal and thrown aside, dumped uglily and sombrely on the landscape, to remain there forever. Each year it grows larger, encroaches further down the vale, a loose sombre little hill. In prosperous times no one takes any notice of it: a dirty, ugly dump. (Davies, 1996c: 267)

Equally 'thrown aside' and 'dumped' are the unemployed miners, who, despite the winter's cold, search among the shifting waste for the bits and pieces of discarded coal that provide heat for their families. They scuttle across the loose stone like beetles and eagerly drag their sacks to each new cartload of waste, for 'there was more promise in a fresh load of rubbish' (ibid.: 268). This ironic 'promise' in the 'fresh' 'rubbish' echoes the general feeling of betrayal: the 'old days, when stomachs were full and people out among the shops with pound-notes in their pockets', has given way to a 'straggling,' 'attenuated' and 'shrunken life in the 'narrow vale' below (ibid.).

Against these dehumanizing conditions, Davies offers the compassionate solidarity of the men, whose communal loyalty easily replaces their competition for the scant resources on the tip. When Gomer Lewis's daughter climbs the tip to announce the birth of Gomer's son, the other men fill his sack from their own supplies so that mother and child will have the warmth they need. As Mog says 'with a determined gaiety, "the young chap'll see a real fire on his first winter's night, as is proper"' (ibid.: 272). There is a great deal that is not 'proper' in the lives of these mining families, Davies suggests, but they are more than the waste and rubbish to which an indifferent industry has reduced them:

> Up on the tip, Mog had followed father and daughter's progress with a troubled mien. His jauntiness had been wiped away for a while; still he was shocked. It seemed to him the most dangerous folly to bring forth young into this world, with times as they were . . . yet . . . He tightened his belt. Why, after all, should the nasty behaviour of the times be allowed to affect a man's true life! Life must proceed. Gomer had a courage which he, Mog, did not possess.
>
> The rain began to slash across the tip, the sodden clouds plunging nearer the dead hills. Mog looked at his diminished sack. He could hear Gwen's exasperated cry when she caught sight of it. But might as well give up now. Cold and wet: the rain spat large icy drops into his face. Mog suddenly lifted his arm and shook his fist menacingly at the heaving sky. He would like to have a fight with someone just then. The world was dirty, untidy, slovenly . . .
>
> Then he uttered a bark of laughter. What was he doing, shaking his fist at the heavens? Threatening God with a black eye? Snatching up his sack of coal he ran carelessly and easily down the tip, ducking

through the whipping rain and flinging a last good-humoured insult to Walt, whose flattened smudge of a nose was pale blue with cold. Three or four searchers, half-hidden in the rain, still combed the tip. (ibid.: 273)

While this resignation before an abstracted source of injustice might not have the practical political clout that we might like, the story's resilient humanity and defiant working-class solidarity suggests a depth of sympathy that cannot be explained entirely in terms of a shallow market opportunism or a queering of homo-social masculinity. Indeed, one must recall that Davies's artistic coming-of-age occurred in the staunchly leftist environs of Charles Lahr's Progressive Bookshop. Further, as we shall see again in Davies's response to the Second World War, for all of the religious and industrial repression of south Wales, Davies admired and respected the working men and women with whom he grew up, and his political sympathies, if they were anywhere, were always with them.

By the end of the 1930s, Davies was dependent upon a literary market that demanded a distinctively Welsh working-class author; however, he identified more personally with the liberated mobility of the artist, and he constantly worked within these market restrictions toward a passionate and creative individuality. Nevertheless, while he felt constrained by the market, and while his grasp of the political realities of working Wales was, as Dai Smith indicates, attenuated and dioramic rather than thorough and analytical (Smith, 2001: 30), Davies was in his own way 'deeply, gravely committed' (Pritchett, 1937: 428) to the working communities of south Wales. For all the repression, waste and failure he depicts, one never feels that industrialism in Wales was simply an unmitigated disaster.

8
'Time and the Welsh mountains'

While much of Davies's fiction dealt with his contemporary industrial Wales, a great deal of Davies's personal and literary imagination resided in the Welsh past. He largely accepted the notion that Wales is composed of two oppositional yet mutually defining worlds: the world of the town and the world of the country. This relationship is the natural outcome of a nation that was, for much of its recent history, paradoxically defined by both sudden industrialization and the passing of a way of life that industrialization supplanted. The Welsh town and the Welsh country have specific spatial and temporal associations. The town is undeniably *in* history. It is an effect of material process and passage through time: it rose with the emergence of industrialization in Wales, and it is headed to an economic collapse, or apocalypse. The country is an eternal space recalling the ancient history and community of Wales; it is pure, clean and untouched by the material forces of history.

This tension runs throughout the Glan Ystrad trilogy. Even *Jubilee Blues*, the most 'industrial' of the three novels, ends with the Lazarus-like rebirth of Cassie Jones as she escapes the Depression-wasted coal-mining village and returns to the rural rhythms of Carmarthenshire:

> She had died and was rising again. She was raw and exposed. Drops of sweat fell down her face; warmth was pounding through her. At the back of her mind she remembered she had a train to catch, and she looked anxiously at the clock in the post-office. Further down, in the main valley, she bought a pound of apples. (Davies, 1938: 315)

The rebirth and the cyclical return to the country, symbolically reinforced by the apples' bounty, undermines the mechanical passage through space and time symbolized by the train and clock. The trilogy ends, therefore by reminding us that Davies almost always imagined his contemporary Wales in the presence of its past.

As Raymond Williams explains, the Welsh past exists alongside the Welsh present in the physical landscape of industrial valleys and untouched mountains:

> The pastoral life, which had been Welsh history, is still another Welsh present, and in its visible presence – not as an ideal contrast, but as the slope, the skyline, to be seen immediately from the streets and from the pit-tops – it is a shape that manifests not only a consciousness of history but a consciousness of alternatives, and then, in a modern form, a consciousness of aspirations and possibilities. The traditional basic contrasts of darkness and light, of being trapped and of getting clear, are here on the ground in the most specific ways, and are the deepest basic movement of all this writing. (Williams, 1980: 223; italics added)

The mountains and their potentially memorial nature are neither ideal contrasts to, nor escapes or elisions of, the working community; on the contrary, they are a dependent alternative underlining the present working conditions – valleys and mountains are not only impossible to separate, they define each other – each constitutive in the other's existence on the border between the past and the present.

In 1946, Davies wrote an essay titled 'Time and the Welsh Mountains'. As the title of the article suggests, Davies perceived the purest form of Wales in temporal and spatial terms, before and away from the industrialization of the South. This essay was part of a collection called *Countryside Character* (1946), and in it Davies assumes a role very similar to the one represented by his 'Britain in Pictures' book, *The Story of Wales*, or the 'My Country' series, anthologizing himself and Wales in a kind of snapshot collection of places. 'Time and the Welsh Mountains' derives from Davies's experiences while spending two days with some farming relations in Carmarthenshire. The experience was an important one for Davies, as it reappeared in several forms throughout his career. Following its appearance in *My Wales* (1937), there were also the very similar examples of Penllyn in *The Perishable Quality* (1957) and Henllys in *Girl Waiting in the Shade* (1960). The experience was also used as the last chapter of *Print of a Hare's Foot* (1969), but Heinemann cut the chapter in the final drafts. It even finds mention in his personal correspondence, when, shortly after his visit to the farm, Davies wrote to Raymond Marriott that he has spent two days in a 'most primitive farm' in which '[l]ife and faces . . . [are] much the same . . . as 500 years ago' (RD to RB 22 October 1936 NLW MS 20897 E 26). This quaint and ancient farm reappears throughout five decades of Davies's writing and represents his continued unwillingness to completely cast off the mantle of the representative Welshman.

In 'Time and the Welsh Mountains', Davies has come to a family farm to which he relocates in north Wales, amid the '[o]ld, old mountains' (Davies, 1946d: 210), and feels 'in the night of this land a living sense of an antiquity that has not changed' (ibid.: 215). It is here that he locates the land of the 'true' Welsh descendants:

> It is in such isolated districts as this, protected by mountains, that the pure racial types are found untarnished by time. Now and again, with a start of recognition, one comes across them in the industrial parts of Wales, but there they have an accidental and almost alien look. Close-packed communal living tends, through the generations, to obliterate the original hallmarks and to produce imitative types belonging solely to the coal-pits, the ironfields and the factories. Sometimes I have sat in houses of this pastoral district and, listening to the antique language and watching the vivid play of expression on these cleanly pure faces, felt time abolished. It was that very day the Roman legions left the fringes of the western land with its strange magic green like the green in a cat's eye. The passing of the centuries is an illusion; Owain Glyndwr is still in the mountains and the alien English soldiers still affrighted by this wild land, with its witches' brew of sudden storms, and by this battling with a magician who consorted with anti-English 'spirits of the vasty deep'. (ibid.: 213)

In this ancient landscape and in these undiluted racial types, Davies finds an abiding Welsh past still holding out against the invasion of an alien industrialism. One might like to argue that this passage represents an anti-colonial perspective if it were not expressive of an English exoticism, coded with English literature and presented as a snapshot within an anthology of *British* landscapes.

The Glan Ystrad trilogy, while intended as a fulfilment of a vogue for political fiction in the 1930s, is rooted in this Welsh past. In particular, *Honey and Bread* sets an elegiac tone for the trilogy as a whole. At the heart of the novel is a rather clichéd love affair between Owen Llewellyn, the older, poetic son of the aristocratic Llewellyn family, and the earthy peasant girl, Bronwen. For Owen, Bronwen represents the eternal youth and beauty of his ancestral lands, and for Bronwen, Owen is 'like a story come true in her life; he was handsome and romantic and gentle' (Davies, 1935: 157). This love affair is set against the sinking of the first mines in Owen's valley and the sale of his family's lands to English mining enterprises.

Not coincidentally, the novel's hero shares his name with the iconic Welsh national hero, and this historical romance joins a hackneyed love-plot with the romantic nationalism of the folk:

> Through this valley ... the invading army of Henry IV. [sic] had passed after being sadly routed by Owain Glyndwr in September 1405. Again, in this fifth invasion, the march had been buffeted and thrashed by the rains and storms called forth by the necromancer Owain, and it was a sad procession that filed back through the proud valley where Cadwgan, Owain's henchman, had whetted his battle-axe in response to the chieftain's call. Up in the fastnesses of the deep dark hills the natives rode in triumph; let the winds scream out of the valley's deep throat, the rains lash in torrent, they were made stronger than the storms, they could sing in wild unison with the winds and delight in the torn heavens. (ibid.: 50)

Our hero, the tubercular Owen, who ultimately dies along with his valley, is the descendant of this proud racial spirit and the novel's defender of the romanticized Welsh past. His love affair with the peasant, Bronwen, representative of the Welsh folk, is a continuation of this noble resistance to the inevitable conquest of his lands.

Owen's need to preserve the land of his forefathers ultimately expresses itself in his obsession for Bronwen and what he regards as her native authenticity and connection to the land. Owen imagines himself as physically linked to the land, and rails against its defilement by the industrial invasion:

> He had laid himself out to become the stones of the house, the pastures, the orchard, the maids and youths, the stock. Romantically and as a poet. He could not turn his possessive hands and eyes away from the beloved place. He could not give it up to those unspeakable marauders. If it were wounded and ravaged, stabbed with girders and ulcerated with pits – then something within him, his own real life-pulse, would die too . . . (ibid.: 106)

What his hands and eyes seek to possess, however, is not the land, but Bronwen, for she, in Owen's words 'is made of our trees and our earth and our songs and our magic' (ibid.: 46). As he explains to his brother, David,

> You . . . you have not right to her, David – no right to judge her, to say a word about her. You can't use her properly! How dare you say she's not plain and not ugly! Of course she's plain. Take her features in turn and each of them, and each can be put to shame by one of your well-bred young women friends. But what of the way she lives, has her being? That is beautiful, David, and that is why she is alive and has appeared here . . . (ibid.)

His passion for Bronwen is not for Bronwen the woman, but for Bronwen the ideal of the land:

> He clung closer to her; he could not tell her all she possessed – and all he perceived in her – but through their mutual touch she would be aware. And he knew that he drew from her vitality and health: in her body was heaped the pure wealth of the earth, and his blood was warmed by it. (ibid.: 132)

Bronwen has a primordial connection to the land. Even her name translates from the Welsh as both 'white breast' and 'white hill', fusing the purity of her body with the purity of the land that Owen defends.

Owen and Bronwen's love replicates the search for the authenticity of the folk. Owen turns away from the new industries threatening his home, from his mother's desire to trade the ancestral home for a metropolitan London life, and from a household overrun by 'modern' music, 'modern' novels, *Frazer's Magazine* and *John Bull*, and looks instead to Bronwen, the inheritor and mainstay of the past. At best, Bronwen is a fetish object of a romantic nationalist. Owen even goes so far as to instruct Bronwen that when they meet she is not to wear 'some horrid stiff best garment' (ibid.: 105), but a 'charming' and 'modest peasant frock' that 'connected her easily to how he thought of her – her body mysterious under a pastoral rag' (ibid.). For him, she is 'a country maid such as were sung in old and sometimes rude ballads' (ibid.: 101).

Ultimately, Owen must make way for the new industrial order that prevails at the end of the novel. However, despite the novel's elegiac tone, one is more aware of the nostalgia that the novel *depicts* than the dynamic forms of industrial life that it *predicts*. One is far more aware of an idyllic past than one is of the mines, the encroaching grey dwellings or the massed variety of human life in Davies's contemporary south Wales. This novel exists for its pastoral landscapes, for its quaint feudal harmony and its colourful cast of picturesque characters, like the gardener, Monday Evans, who 'looked evil in a sub-human fashion, a throw-back to the dirt and squalor of the worst tribes that at one time infested the local hills . . . a smelly old satyr about the gardens [giving] the place a reminiscence of former dark ages' (ibid.: 107); or Alias Morris, a pagan landowner and 'dirty man who . . . had the blood of princes in his veins, ancient fighting princes who made his country proud' (ibid.: 114); or 'the witch Rebecca' (ibid.: 236), who emits a 'wild wailing chant in the Welsh language . . . recognized as a witch's curse' (ibid.: 297); or Robert ab Gruffydd, 'the local prophet' (ibid.: 326), living in his 'stinking hut far up the mountain' (ibid.), who still 'possessed a mysterious power' (ibid.), and who speaks out against the mines and agitates the workers to resist the new regime that has no place for such as he. Whatever else it does, *Honey and Bread* provides something very much along the lines of works by Anna Maria Bennett and Allen Raine – books in which 'Welsh scenery is invariably much admired, Welsh harpists, druids, bards, folk customs, and folk music praised, and the simple manners of the people extolled – though not their language' (Aaron, 1995b: 35). It is the story of the thwarted love of a simple girl and a princely boy set against an exotic and picturesque Wales.

With such a strong commitment to this quaint and romantic Welsh past, Davies is never completely able to leave his national themes behind, even when writing in the 1930s of the more international commitments of labour. *A Time to Laugh*, the second novel in the Glan Ystrad trilogy, describes the emergent labour movement in Wales. In the face of the novel's admission of an increasing racial diversity in the valleys (Davies, 1937b: 7), Davies still resorts to the 'pure' racial heritage of the Welsh past. When the novel's middle-class protagonist, Dr Tudor Morris, delivers a speech to a gathering of miners, he does so in the shadow of the Welsh past: 'The valley at night always tasted of ancient things, the mountains seemed to remember unruly tribes, long ago battles, druidical circles of brooding men waiting for the moon' (ibid.: 242). And, in the name of just such a past, he calls the miners to action: 'Men, get yourselves into proper union and remember that as our forefathers fought for the valleys against the thieving barons of old, so we've got to fight, but in a different way, for a different reason' (ibid.). The miners are moved by a 'tribal' (ibid.: 348) and 'savage' ancestry more than by a united commitment to labour.

Along with this Welsh racial heritage, *A Time to Laugh* consistently recalls the bucolic past that preceded it in *Honey and Bread*. It ends with the same New Year rituals that opened and closed *Honey and Bread*, and provides several backward glances to the simpler age underwriting the labour revolts. We find Tudor invoking the lost world of *Honey and Bread* in ballads sung to a now elderly Bronwen:

> Tudor sat at the piano, at Bronwen's request, and sang in his easy baritone gay old Welsh songs of the pre-Nonconformist era: she liked to be reminded now and again of the old bucolic world, when there had not been all this complicated industrial strife. (ibid.: 337)

A Time to Laugh is only an abstracted narrative of labour which never truly escapes the past that Davies imagines so vividly throughout his writing, and which fulfills a popular demand more than a political one, complete with a happy ending, a happily married doctor and his collier's-sister wife, and a happy Welsh peasantry/labour force celebrating on top of the mountain in the security of their ancient customs: 'Far away on the mountain-top at the head of the valley big flames leapt, golden and red. They lit up the green earth, they licked the stars. Small figures, aboriginal-looking, leaping about its glow. There was wild singing down in the valley' (ibid.: 428). Davies's Wales, even at its most 'proletarian', is, like that of Richard Llewellyn, aptly described as 'industrial pastoral'. Whatever 'complicated industrial strife' (ibid.: 337) may afflict Davies's characters, they are always shored up by an abiding Welsh national 'heritage'.

9
'Strange embraces' and 'subtle pagan secrets'

It is fair to condemn Davies for the essentially racist underpinnings of his Welsh past (Bohata, 2001; Williams, 2001; Brown, 2001). It is also fair to condemn Davies for producing an exotic Wild Wales that panders to an essentially English colonial gaze. There has certainly been a long tradition of such novels (Aaron, 1995a; Aaron, 1995b; Rhydderch, 1997). However, Davies's deployment of the Welsh past was not solely racist or market driven, for it also had a deep personal significance. His exotic and primitive Wales was an essential homecoming, achieved through inventing a nationalism unfettered by the rigid industrial Nonconformist sexual codes of Welshness. As Tony Brown points out, this revision of the Welsh past puts flesh on a landscape that still remembers the pre-industrial past and so enables the desires that the industrial, Nonconformist present condemns. As Brown puts it, Davies longs for

> a Wales in which the life of the body and the senses, including presumably the sexual instincts, were not suppressed but seen as related to the rhythms and impulses of the natural world, a life from which Wales had been exiled by the coming of the mechanical world of industrialism and the moral constraints of Nonconformity. (Brown, 2001: 74)

One must, therefore, read Davies's popular Welsh romances in terms of his less marketable need to identify with Wales as a gay man. As Davies wrote *Honey and Bread*, he complained in a letter to G. H. West of what he saw as the absence of homosexual literature:

'I wish someone would write a non-hysterical and straightforward – unfrightened – novel on this subject – difficult, though, so little precedent stuff to guide and aid one; it's a raw subject in literature' (RD to GHW 7 February 1934 HRHRC). He had just read Stephen Spender's 'By the Lake', and found it 'curiously arresting, though only half-told, like all these homosexual stories' (RD to GHW 7 February 1934 HRHRC). Davies wrote this while writing a novel that, however pandering to popular English tastes it might have been in its superficial trappings, also contained an obvious queer subtext that, although only 'half-told', underwrites the popular themes with a personal narrative of sexual liberation.

Owen, despite his love for Bronwen, is one of Davies's most queered male characters. His devotion to Bronwen is aesthetic and patriotic rather than physically passionate, and the novel indulges in a recurring anxiety regarding Owen's unusual and possibly abnormal nature, particularly with regard to his gender identifications. Specifically, Davies imbues Owen with a 'streak of feminine perception' (Davies, 1935: 65), a general lack of interest in women, and homoerotic sympathies and relationships that together work towards a queered vision of the Welsh past. Inevitably, this homosexual must die, as the new industrial, religious and economic forms of life emerge.

As discussed earlier, Owen's love for Bronwen has little to do with his love of her body. Indeed, when he denies his unambiguously masculine brother access to Bronwen, he removes her from the realm of heterosexual exchange, not only by denouncing her attractiveness, but by insisting that David would not know 'how to use her' (ibid.: 46) and has 'no right to her' (ibid.). She is a sexualization of the land, but she does not strongly *hetero*sexualize Owen. Owen is, further, like so many of Davies's queer characters, a bit of a dandy, who contrasts with his more businesslike and practical brother. He is like many of Davies's dandies, whose sexualities are removed into some aesthetic abstraction, be it art, clothing or dramatic performance. Owen's idealized vision of Bronwen is no different, and Davies goes to great lengths to demonstrate Owen's lack of interest in women. When Owen asks that his brother, David, keep away from Bronwen, his brother notes that Owen had 'never liked [girls] until this one' (ibid.: 33). The subsequent women he encounters get very short shrift. In one instance, he recognizes two sisters as pretty, but 'stiff and cool as porcelain'. They are 'charming to look at, but a little painful to think about' (ibid.: 91–2). In another instance, Owen dismisses the five daughters of a family friend as 'grotesque', 'ugly' 'monsters' (ibid.: 194). When Owen sees these women 'bearing down on [him] from a cliff', he collapses upon the beach (ibid.: 195). Owen apparently shares the 'unfortunate' trait of one of his ancestors, who was afflicted with a 'strange horror of women' (ibid.: 56).

These women who elicit Owen's horror are the refined daughters of wealthy families and are, therefore, devoid of the romantic ideal embodied in Bronwen. In her connection to the land, Bronwen is a proxy for an ideal classless world steeped in a magical paganism of possibility:

> Owen was thinking how fire at night, amid trees and under a wintry sky, made the blood long for incantations, strange embraces, and the processes of magic. What had been lost, what subtle pagan secrets? . . . The magical fire: its burning warmed him. And he watched Bronwen as the flames, devouring the heart of the wood, leapt in a last frenzy to the heavens. (ibid.: 42)

Owen's longing for 'strange embraces' and 'subtle pagan secrets' indicates desires that are strange, subtle and secret. These defiantly Welsh erotic landscapes redraw the boundaries of sexual identification and open the Welsh borders to Davies's queerness.

In Bronwen, we see that the eroticization of the pre-industrial landscape swings both ways, as it were. The exotic Welsh past allows for much more fluid erotic geographies, even as it fixes Wales in idyllic national permanence. The same may be said of Owen. When Owen's father hears of his son's affair with Bronwen, he is pleased to discover that '[t]he boy had normal interests after all' (ibid.: 240). This abnormality derives not only from Owen's general aversion to women, but from the large measures of femininity perceived in his nature. David observes that sometimes Owen talks 'as though [he] were [David's] elder sister' rather than his elder brother, to which observation Owen replies, 'I know, . . . Oddly enough, that's how I feel sometimes' (ibid.: 72). Further, when David tells Owen that their mother thought that she should have had a daughter instead of Owen, Owen criticizes his mother as 'unsubtle' (ibid.: 79). This response recalls those 'subtle pagan secrets' (ibid.: 42) and begs the question, what 'subtle' sexuality is Davies trying to implant within this character? It would seem that Owen resists the simple reduction of his nature to either masculine or feminine. Davies has elsewhere expressed the belief that the male artist cannot afford to be entirely masculine (Davies, 1997: 139; Jones, 1996: 12), and he may simply be granting Owen the sensitivity of the artist. At the time of the novel's publication, those large measures of femininity in Owen would probably have been read in this light, their threat diffused by his consummation (in this case, not simply masturbatory) of his love for Bronwen. However, the cumulative picture of Owen that emerges is of an 'abnormal' and 'odd' man, whose oddness is intimately connected to his troubling relationship to gender.

The discomfort surrounding Owen's nature reaches its climax in his defence of two ganders who have a 'mortal fear' of geese, and who choose instead to squat alone together 'in delightful white peace' (Davies, 1935: 80–1). The ganders' keeper, Evan, is enraged at the birds, damning them as 'wicked' and 'Heathens', but Owen is touched by the 'eccentric' ganders and what he regards as their 'faithful' marriage (ibid.: 80–2). When Evans determines to 'lock them up separate' to 'punish them', Owen advises him that he will fail to 'cure' the ganders, because 'Nature is very strange on occasion . . . She doesn't always behave as men expect her to. It seems that she likes to tease us sometimes' (ibid.: 82). He therefore solemnly advises Evan to 'leave the poor ganders to themselves . . . [because they] seem so content with each other' (ibid.). While illustrated in the comic love of two ganders, this incident resists disciplinary efforts to lock up and cure 'deviant' sexualities. Owen denaturalizes nature and opens up a space of possibility for eccentric sexual identities that do not revolve around typically stable and 'unsubtle' constructions of gender.

The authority implied in Evan's disciplinary presence is turned upon Owen as well. Mrs Vaughan, a wealthy neighbour and matchmaker to her nieces, decides that whenever Owen is about there is 'something not quite decent in the air' (ibid.: 91). She is troubled by a 'strange lawlessness' (ibid.: 88) in the young man that she is unable to name: 'A difficult and strange young man, was Tudor Llewellyn's elder son. *Not quite* . . . she fumbled in her mind . . . well not *quite* – She gave it up' (ibid.). Owen escapes her terms of definition and is, ultimately, characterized by the conspicuous silence surrounding most of Davies's queer characters. Mrs Vaughan satisfies herself by recognizing him simply as indecent, but not before she passes her death sentence on the ganders, which Owen describes to her in vain as comparable to David and Jonathan.

Owen, it seems, does not quite belong here, but then neither, presumably, does the industrial labour that is about to alter not only the romantic landscape of the valley and its traditional forms of life (and the myth of a coherent national past), but, throughout the subsequent novels of the trilogy, the generic preoccupations of the novel as well. A figure like Owen is increasingly impossible in the ostensible working-class narratives of *A Time to Laugh* and *Jubilee Blues*. So, beneath the conventional love-plot of *Honey and Bread* one finds an insurgent sexuality, resisting what Davies regards as the increasingly limited identity positions of modern life through the invocation of an imaginary pagan and libertine Welsh past. Through Owen, Davies invents a Wales that does not exclude the 'strange embraces' of gay sexuality.

Nor is this linking of a liberated sexuality with the romantic and exotic Welsh past limited to *Honey and Bread*. *The Black Venus* (1944), Davies's most successful novel in terms of sales, is implicated in the secret loves of the closeted homosexual seeking release from the 'civilized' and static manners that keep him chained to a respectable heterosexuality. One might even go so far as to argue that the novel's central motif, courting in bed, closely replicates Davies's own sexual subterfuge as a lodger. In typically oblique fashion, Davies recalls one incident in early London years when 'Giving sanctuary one night – secretly of course – to a hazy friend, [his] rickety bed collapsed under [them], two of its legs dissolving and the wire underlay tearing from its frame. Rid of [his] friend without detection in the morning, [he] summoned the landlady to view the wreck' (Davies, 1998; 115). Essentially, when Olwen, the central character of *The Black Venus*, publicly demands her right to sexual supremacy in the private bedroom, she performs Davies's anxious desire for a sexuality unfettered by codes of silence and surveillance.

This sexual freedom is equally evident in the second of two Black Venuses depicted in the novel. The canopy of Olwen's four-poster bed displays 'a marine design of fishes, shells, boats and anchors, with as centrepiece, for no reason at all, a buxom young negress holding up a large key' (Davies, 1944a: 73). The iconography of empire, slavery and colonial oppression is painfully obvious, but the key has multiple symbolic referents. It symbolizes access to Olwen's room, her bed and her sexuality, which she, and no man, holds. In the context of the excessive sexualization of the negress (Bohata, 2001), however, the key might also symbolize the phallus of the one man who will inevitably claim his prize. Lastly, it also suggests things hidden and locked away, which, in its association with the bed and the private space of the bedroom, again refers to Davies's homosexuality. Like Lawrence and Nancy Cunard, two of his early influences in terms of racial and racist representation, Davies deploys authentic 'primitive' sexuality as a potentially liberating one that will release Olwen from the chains of traditional domesticity. The imagery of chains recurs throughout the novel, and Olwen is determined to cast them off:

> A new century we are in. But still are women locked up. Shocking it is to admit that they *want* to be locked up. Why is this? Because no better they know and because the cramp of their chains is still in their

limbs. Only harlots and not nice women are free, but outcasts they are from the hearth, the chapel and the social meeting and therefore worthless for our consideration . . . (Davies, 1944a: 41)

That 'harlots' and 'not nice women' are the only ones who are free is important. Equally important is that Olwen does not condemn these women, whose 'deviant' sexualities seem to exist on a continuum with her own defiance of custom, even though it threatens exile from hearth and home.

This defiant call for an eccentric reclamation of home returns us to Brown's contention that Davies's primitive and tribal Wales is part of a return home for the exiled Welsh queer. At the end of Olwen's defiant campaign, her resistance is articulated against the modern/English moral invasion, and she becomes a spokesperson, not just for liberated women, but for the nobility of the more pagan and liberal Welsh past, prevailing against the modernizing influences threatening the pastoral perfection of this novelized Wales:

> Perhaps it was true that a wide-awake person could bow to those laws and yet outwit them. Was not that the whole secret of a successful life? And was not the body always chained, but only real slaves allowed their minds to be imprisoned? . . . She could be like her native country. It was a conquered territory obedient to the material sovereignty of an alien race. But still the old wild soul of Wales pulsed triumphantly within her borders – and here and there, like the tenacious Jewish stock, outside them also. (ibid.: 297)

This is a complex passage pointing to many of Davies's conflicts. The conflation of the sexual resistance and the national one is particularly telling in its illumination of the sexual nature of Davies's expatriation from Wales and his longing to return to a more liberal (and pagan) Welsh past, even as he lives outside Welsh borders. His treatment of chains recalls words written just a year earlier in *The Story of Wales*, where Davies describes Welsh subservience to England as one cause of the Welsh independence of spirit: 'Chains are curious things. They can be made to vanish while still about one, they can develop inward resources, they can blossom like the pilgrim's staff' (Davies, 1943b: 8). Read in the context of *The Black Venus* and of Davies's closeted queerness, these words seem to speak to the hegemony of hetero-normativity, just as much as they do to Welsh subservience to England. They also remind us of the futility of 'locking up' the 'wicked' ganders in *Honey and Bread* and Davies's own subversion of the authority of border guards. In Olwen, and in the similarly named Owen of *Honey and Bread*, Davies creates a nationality that is racially coded as both authentically Welsh and authentically erotic, in opposition to the modern moralities that were imported with an alien modernization.

10
'One's own interior liberty'

The Glan Ystrad trilogy was finished in 1938 and *The Black Venus* was published in 1944, yet, particularly with regard to *The Black Venus*, one would think that the Second World War had not occurred. The truth is that the war depressed Davies a great deal, and he found himself drifting between escapism and engagement, just as he found himself moving between the wartime industries of Blaenclydach, the rural escape of Henley and the falling walls of London. By the end of the war, his typical homelessness became even more pronounced, and he explained that he could not 'foresee any real settled abode for [himself] until after the war', for he was 'in an interior turmoil – full of hatred for the world and the way it's going' (RD to LQ 5 November 1944 NLW MS 20897 E 45).

But this drifting and this movement is not only a brief symptom of the war, for this period also marked a significant change in direction in Davies's career. At this time, he not only began to move away from stories and novels set in working-class Rhondda but also accepted that the bohemian literary world where he made his name no longer existed. Both of these changes are marked most dramatically by the destruction of Charles Lahr's Progressive Bookshop during the Blitz in 1941. While Davies remained a faithful friend to the Lahrs and a frequent visitor to the various unsuccessful bookshops held by Lahr after the war, this vibrant forum of leftist debate and artistic adventure presided over by its stateless anarchist patron had passed into the oblivion of international furies.

Davies spent most of the war years outside London, apart from occasional visits and a brief stint working in the War Office between July and December of 1942. His age and a grade IV medical category had kept him from any more rigorous duties. He was more comfortable, it seemed, in Henley with Vincent, or visiting Louis Quinain in Shamley Green, or in Blaenclydach, where he lived for most of 1941. This physical removal from London runs parallel with an imaginative retreat from the war.

The disengagement evident in the romantic folk atmosphere of *The Black Venus* is preceded by Davies's flight to the mountains of rural Wales in a story of dark and secret passion, *Under the Rose* (1940). This novel, while set in Wales, takes place in a rural fastness and revolves around the thwarted passions of a spinster, Rachel Lloyd, a descendant of one of the old families of the county. The novel opens with the return of Rachel's girlhood lover, Stephen Meredith, who had abandoned her on the eve of their wedding. In vengeance, she murders Stephen in her parlour with a bread knife and buries him in the garden beneath her prize-winning roses. The rest of the novel follows Rachel as she tries in vain to recapture her lost youth. When Stephen's city lover traces him to Rachel's house, she guesses Rachel's crime and blackmails her. The novel ends with Rachel's eventual madness, and she jumps to her death from a mountain height. In its background and primary themes, this was not the Wales that people had come to expect from Davies. It did not have those 'growls and barking' of *A Time to Laugh* and *Jubilee Blues*, nor even the dark historical prophecies of *Honey and Bread*.

When the first reviews appeared, Davies felt that he had been told to keep in his place, and wrote as much to friend and theatre critic Raymond Marriott:

> Yes, 'Under the Rose' bloomed last Monday – but so far only its thorn has been evident. Did you see yesterday [*sic*] 'Observer', or the 'Times Lit. Supp'? Such rebuke! It seems that it's not for me to deal in dark murders. This is what one gets for exploring new avenues? (RD to RM 23 September 1940 NLW MS 20897 E)

As Davies later explained to Marriott, these 'new avenues' were too far from his working-class ones: 'As far as I can judge, people think I ought not to have left the woes of the workers to write this kind of book. A pox on such limited minds' (RD to RM undated NLW MS 20897 E 49). When Raymond Marriott finally read the novel and did not like it, Davies responded in a somewhat reflexive tone:

> Sorry you didn't like *Under the Rose*. It was the product of Rhys Davies no 2, who is not necessarily inferior to no 1, only different. I have a side of me which must be expressed in that type of work. But what I ought to do, of course, is to have two names (like Wm Sharp and Fiona Macleod – wasn't it?). (RD to RM April 1941 NLW MS 20897 E 52)

Davies expresses the same sentiment to George Bullock, another critic and Marriott's gay partner:

> I must say that (if this war hadn't taken such a serious turn?) I thought [*Under the Rose*] would stand a chance of selling. Also I had one eye on stage and screen. But, alas, I'm beginning to see that it's not in me to write a best seller. As I wrote it I began to forget the bloody public and became entirely absorbed in it <u>for myself</u>. (RD to GB July/Aug 1940 HRHRC)

This self-centred artistic retreat is replicated in Davies's own reading material at the time. Melville's *Moby Dick* and *Typee* offer him 'an escape from our world: refreshing whilst one reads, but to return to our day so melancholy' (RD to RM 21 May 1940 NLW MS 20897 E 45). Kate O'Brien had the same reaction to *Under the Rose*, which, as she explained in her *Spectator* review, took her 'mind refreshingly away during many hours from actual, international furies to those, more satisfactorily purging, of the imagination and the individual' (O'Brien, 1940: 348). She did not agree, then, with Daniel George's *Tribune* review, which accused Davies of promoting a feminine idleness:

> The reading public of the last twenty years or so has consisted very largely of the middle-class women who live in the suburbs in a state

of robust idleness, their small families taken off their hands by nurses and their houses efficiently run by servants ... That enfeebling influence will cease. Women will have to work harder and, if the war is of long duration, they will have to bear more children. The world will become harder, and hard people will want books written with power about important things. (George, 1940: 16)

Davies, George explains, fails to do so.

As if in response to George and the other critics, Davies's next novel, *Tomorrow to Fresh Woods* (1941), returned to the Rhondda. Rather than turn away from the political realities of the war, Davies felt the novel was an answer to them:

The last chapter is sort of looking forward (desperately?) to some sort of belief, though in a quite unsentimental way – I <u>do</u> realize we're in for some horrors and there are going to be periods of intense disgusts. But I feel we've got to <u>believe</u> in something better. Otherwise it's best to be dead. (RD to RM 3 July 1941 NLW MS 20897 E 54)

In the final section, titled 'The Undefeated', Penry returns to a home-town whose labour leaders have been defeated and whose colliery is on the verge of closure, but, in the words of 'All to Pieces Dai', the town collapses into the fullness of its life:

To Wern I came before it was, and by here I am now that it's going. A bit responsible for it I am feeling – ay, myn ufferni, a load on my back it is. Standing by here for fifty years I been and seen the hool place pass up and down, and often asking myself, 'What's it all for?' Thousands sweating their insides out, working and marrying and christening and burying, and brides in their white and preachers in their black, and socialists shouting their jaws crooked on this corner, and policemen's heads split open in the riots, and the Male Voice Choir going up to Pisgah chapel to practise for the Eisteddfod – (Davies, 1941: 298)

He stops mid speech to listen to the coming night at the end of an era of coal, and he proclaims that the nightingale has returned to

Wern. And in the final chapter, as Penry looks down on Wern, he too hears a note of hope:

> 'Look at it! Sometimes when I've seen it from the mountaintops in the clear light of day, I've thought, can one have faith in a people that could build a place like that – or tolerate living in it? Then I've thought how magnificent that they've come through – the people – that they've kept fighting, though often they've scarcely known what they were fighting for! Something blind surging up . . . And when I heard them singing to-day in the Wern Inn after the funeral, I thought, they're rich, they're still rich with life . . . And I went into the pub for a few minutes' – he began laughing – 'and heard All to Pieces Dai give a little speech. Do you know what the old waster said? – "Nothing can kill us except death!" To me he seemed to be the voice of a race unconsciously celebrating the close of an era'. (ibid.: 312)

This novel ends in the 1930s, when the rumblings of the Second World War can be heard just over the horizon, and Davies's celebration of defiant human life, persevering in spite of the grinding inhuman forces of industry, corresponds closely with his fear and defiance of the war machine that was grinding up young bodies as he wrote the novel.

As much as Davies longed to retreat from the war, he was very engaged with it imaginatively. As early as 1936, sitting down before the daily papers in Henley presented a grim prospect, as he explained to Raymond Marriott: 'I can't bear to read the papers until after lunch. Hitler's cow eyes on one page. Mussolini's misshapen mug on another, Spanish doings on the next. Horrors!' (RD to RM 7 September 1936 NLW MS 20897 E 24). He continues to Marriott in the same vein, as he writes again from Henley on almost the eve of Britain's entrance into the war:

> What a fascist racket. I'm ashamed of humanity. I try to keep balanced by feeling nothing but contempt and indifference for the whole sordid business, but the worst of it is one <u>cannot</u> be aloof. Not with the threat of bombs falling about one. My instinct seems to say there'll be no war, but when I read the newspapers the utmost gloom descends on me. (RD to RM 30 August 1939 NLW MS 20897 E 37)

When the war does arrive, Davies feels that it has destroyed the London in which he grew into his artistic maturity, and claims that he cannot imagine creating in this condition of widespread destruction:

> I'm beginning not to miss London, since <u>my</u> London no longer exists. The wisest course for such as us (if one can do it) is to turn one's back on the war – imaginatively speaking – and isolate oneself in some outlandish place, as D. H. Lawrence did in the last war. When the great bestial War Machine is in action writers are of no use whatsoever, its activities, which are destructive, are in complete opposition to them. If they do write on the subject of War – <u>While it's being waged</u> – their stuff is terribly feeble, useless and unrecognizable. Their time comes afterwards – 'emotion remembered in tranquility' sort of thing. (RD to RM 26 February 1941 NLW MS 20897 E 51)

Although he claimed that he was 'not going to write any more books while the war is on' (RD to RM July 3 1941 NLW MS 20897 E 54), Davies wrote three novels, two collections of short stories, a biography and the topographical picture-book *The Story of Wales*, all between 1940 and 1946. As mentioned, some of these works, like *Under the Rose* and *The Black Venus*, represent a significant retreat from the political realities of wartime Europe, but others offer a direct imaginative engagement with them.

'Boy With a Trumpet' (1949) represents the latter vein, and reflects the despair that characterizes Davies's wartime letters. In this story, a fallen angel Gabriel fails to blow the triumphant horn at the end of the world. The central figure is a young and simple orphan, who has been damaged by the war, kicked out of the army and left to wander aimlessly through the bombed-out streets of London, his only treasure a shiny second-hand trumpet that he can barely play. He ends up in a boarding house for prostitutes, where the 'calm acceptance of the world as disintegration eased him' (Davies, 1996b: 100). The indifferent human contact in the house pleases him, for it 'belonged to the chaos, the burnt-out world reduced to charcoal' (ibid.: 101), and he wonders what would happen if he blew his horn on the night-time staircase 'over the fallen night, waken these dead, surprise them with a new anarchial fanfare?' (Davies, 1996b: 101).

However, he ends up abandoning his trumpet when the Guards Sergeant, Harry, full of vital manhood, plays the 'Londonderry Air' like an 'announcement of the lifted sun' (ibid.: 102). Harry plays with more skill than the boy will ever have, and thereby robs him of his belief in his power to redeem the world. He now sees only a world of crime, for 'you can't do so much killing, so much teaching to destroy, and then stop it suddenly' (ibid.: 103). To the old crimes will be added 'new crimes against the holiness of the heart. There'll be fear, and shame, and guilt, guilt. People will be mad. There's no such thing as victory in war. There's only misery, chaos and suffering for everybody, and then the payment' (ibid.). Alone at the end of the story, he looks over bombed-out London, whose wasted devastation has become a hellscape for the lost souls of a new age:

> He saw a grey dead light falling over smashed cities, over broken precipices and jagged torn chasms of the world. Acrid smoke from abandoned ruins mingled with the smell of blood. He saw himself the inhabitant of a wilderness where withered hands could lift in guidance no more. There were no more voices and all the paps of the world were dry. (ibid.: 104)

In this passage, and in the story as a whole, we get a sense of the London that Davies has lost. The London that he arrived in as a young man to begin making a living as an artist is gone, and with it, all hope for the future.

An earlier story of the London Blitz, 'Spectre de la Rose' (1945), shares with 'Boy With a Trumpet' its sense of imminent disintegration. It opens in a blacked-out Soho pub that is tense with a strained joviality. The 'knots' of 'crimped', 'cracked' and 'battered' people keep up a 'brittle chatter' (Davies, 1996c: 315) to fend off the knowledge that the world is falling apart around them. At the bar, and at the heart of the story, sits one of Davies's more grotesque portraits:

> A thin painted spectre, she sat alone with a Guinness before her, sat bolt upright within her sad fleshless bones, her fragile fingers tapering into long blue nails. She was like a chalky drawing in pale pinks, blues and evanescent whites. Wan pearls hung about her stringy neck. On her shady old-style hat was pinned a single ornamentation – a large faded artificial rose. Yet there was something jaunty about that sentimental pink rose. It sailed the air with a kind of romantic bravado, and gave an added horror to the falling structure of the face beneath. That face contained a nostril half-eaten away; a rat might have been at it. (ibid.: 316–17)

Reminiscent of Edgar Degas's *Absinthe Drinker* (1876), this description echoes that painting's sense of listless failure at the heart of metropolitan confidence. The woman sits at the bar like the lingering corpse of dying age, dwindling and fading away, her face falling like the 'falling structures' of the London buildings. Yet, in the eyes of Nick, the central sentimental character of the story, she represents a barely abiding glory, with her pearls and her faded but undying rose.

To Nick, the spectre belongs to a more beautiful world that the war is blasting out of existence. As she sits in the bar she smiles vaguely at the 'young folly around her' (ibid.: 321), and the fires following the air raid embody her spirit's happy departure from humanity's latest madness: 'A rosy light skipped the streets and leapt over the rooftops, a pink-gold jump of radiance distributing like blown petals wide into the sky' (ibid.: 322). She steps aside before the 'mathematical obscurity' (ibid.: 321) of the bombs, and she fades away in the face of the dull menacing reality of the anti-aircraft guns and bombers:

> But the din outside had risen, crash upon crash, the hot soar of the shells, the intolerant explosions in air, cleansing the sky of its scudding monstrous beetles, god-images of man's last masochism. They were above, above. Up there concise little men garbed in neutral grey looked down with remote curiosity at a breaking world. In their fire-garlanded cars they were young gods alien to the sentimental womb of the earth. They looked down without gloating, precisely fulfilling a sick creed. (ibid.: 321)

This magnificent passage of technological sublimity reverses the heavenly reach of progress without diminishing its splendour, and its vital destruction inverts the spectre's wasted vitality.

In defiance of this indifferent destruction of the present, Nick enters the churchyard of St Anne's in search of Hazlitt's grave. The trees are filled with clothing, 'as if the interred, thumped out of their silence by this second assault, had found their cerements too heavy for their ethereal flight' (ibid.: 322), and Nick finds the grave intact. His musing reminder of Hazlitt's belief in 'the theoretical benevolence and the practical malignity of man' (ibid.: 323) recalls an earlier period of war and apocalypse. This spectral scene of the memorialized dead signals a qualified connection to an imperishable past, symbolically reinforced by a wondering appreciation for a second-hand dance-hall frock of silk: 'It's funny, . . . [a] blast will puff a house down to the ground and blow a body into nothing, but often . . . it won't destroy silk' (ibid.). One hopes that something will survive the devastation, and that the more ethereal (or more spectral) a thing is, the harder it is to destroy. Both 'Boy With a Trumpet' and 'Spectre de la Rose' nicely capture Davies's response to the Second World War. The fallen tuneless trumpet and the desperate search for Hazlitt's grave figure the challenges of finding meaning in wartime and postwar devastation.

More personally for Davies, the bombs falling on London had destroyed the site of his personal liberation. Indeed, the greatest threat that Davies perceived was that posed to the individual creative imagination:

> I see that even the papers don't play the 'democracy versus fascism' pedal so often now. What people don't seem to realize is that there's been a real revolution in England the last three or four months, and now we're as fascist as any country – in this Hitler has already been victorious here . . . We shall have to evolve, to meet this, a new personal philosophy. I'm [one] of those who believe that nothing on earth can impair one's own interior liberty – unless you allow it to. Though outwardly bothered and vexed, I have reached a certain calm. (RD to GB July 1, 1940 HRHRC)

Davies is no doubt referring to the continuing activities of Oswald Mosley's British Union of Fascists, but his reaction against rising Fascist regimes in Europe began at least as early as a trip to Germany in the late 1920s and early 1930s, where he witnessed the nascent forms of Nazism. Recalling these trips in *Print of a Hare's Foot*, he opposes the homogenizing authority of Fascist Germany to the late stage of Berlin libertinism. In Cologne, he was 'held up' by 'a gigantic procession of Brownshirts' and '[o]nly the sharp tramp of boots could be heard in the docile quiet. Phalanx after phalanx marched with magnificent precision, endless columns of curt-faced men, all alike in expression' (Davies, 1997: 161). However, in Berlin shortly after this sight, he drank in the Eldorado nightclub with various queers and transvestites. Here, one transvestite explains that while he and his partner travelled across Europe as husband and wife, he changed into men's clothes when 'arriving at a frontier' (ibid.: 162). When the luggage was examined, the guards stared 'at all [his] frocks and [his] three wigs, but they're used to everything' (ibid.). The contrast between the fluidly performed identities of the Eldorado and the rigidly restrictive authority of the Brownshirts is reinforced by the anxiety over selfhood on the frontier, illustrating how deeply personal were the political fears that European Fascism engendered in Davies.

Nevertheless, this bewigged feminized luggage also maintains Davies's agile and comic subversion of uniformed authority of all kinds, like his camp resistance to enlisting: 'I suppose by rights I ought to be in khaki, but I hate it as a colour' (RD to RM 21 May 1940 NLW MS 23106 E 1). And while Davies was unwilling to put uniforms on, he was more than happy to remove them, exercising his 'own interior liberty' with normally regimented bodies:

> I discovered, after all, two 'sinks of iniquity' – a couple of 'gayish' pubs, rather low, where the local military and RAF foregathered for sing-songs etc, with a sprinkling of their good-hearted, apple-cheeked, if boisterous, wenches. I sang with them – folk songs, old ballads, hymns etc etc. I met an amusing RAF boy from Yorkshire, very camp. Also two bits of native nonsense (while the moon was shining), one of

which knew London very well indeed. As you may guess, I was last off the promenade at night'. (RD to LQ Friday 19 September 1941 NLW MS 23106 E 13)

This sexually coded playfulness with militarism offers an inversion of the Fascist assault on personal liberty that Davies witnessed in Germany and feared in the eyes of dictators, staring at him from the pages of the daily papers.

A more focused attack on the Fascist threat to individual liberty is found in 'Cherry-Blossom on the Rhine', a short story that circulated in several periodicals in three languages before its inclusion in Davies's 1936 collection, *The Things Men Do*. In this story, a young English girl, Louie, listlessly seeks an authentic romantic encounter to inject life into a vacation grown stale, due to her mother's guidebook tourism. The young *Wandervögel* who catches her eye during a visit to St Goar is very obligingly named Siegfried, yet the free-spirited wandering of the *Wandervögel* has transformed into the nationalist strictures of the Hitler *Jugend*. Sneaking out into the night with the young man, Louie quickly discovers that the erotic possibility of their moonlit tryst is impossible in the new Germany. Declaring that 'love is international' (Davies, 1996a: 138), Siegfried praises Louie's pale skin, white as the cherry-blossom, and compares her to the sylphs and fairies of German myth and legend, but Louie defies an 'international' love that is mired in the Fascist nationalism of the German past.

This story offers a compelling counterpoint to Davies's own appeals to racially pure pasts, for Louie's defiance quickly turns subversive, and she upsets Siegfried's belief in her racial purity by informing him of her Jewish great-grandmother. Uneasily, Siegfried accommodates the stain of impure blood, but the cracks are now showing. One can no longer ignore the fact that the song of the Lorelei, with which Siegfried adorns the Rhineland landscape and romanticizes Louie's femininity, was written by Heinrich Heine, a German Jew. The story therefore undermines the very notion of purity, presenting it as something that is inevitably artificial. This artificiality is further signalled in Siegfried's appeal to the storied Lorelei rock, the legendary romance of which is reduced in Louie's eyes to the hollowness of her mother's guidebook mania for scenery. When Siegfried suggests that a woman should be placed upon the rock, Louie mockingly carries the idea to its absurd logical conclusion: 'And she could wear a wig with hair down to her feet . . . And when there's no moonlight, coloured electric lamps around the rock' (ibid.: 139).

Ultimately, Siegfried's love is far from 'international', for it draws more borders than it removes. Before she leaves Siegfried, Louie refuses to be defined in terms of Siegfried's artificial purity; alternatively, she co-opts his condemnation of cosmetic beauty into an aesthetic power of creative self-fashioning:

> 'I'm not wholesome,' she mocked, dragging her fingers away from him. 'And I like my clothes from Paris, not cut out of a banner on the Rhine. And in the morning I shall always use rose-red lipstick, and in the evening magenta. And your love is *not* international.' (ibid.: 142)

Louie's dismissal of Siegfried's 'purity' is a typically aesthetic dismissal of nature. She maintains that her rose-red lipstick is truer than Siegfried's white cherry-blossoms, for in not pretending to be singularly 'authentic', she accesses a greater human freedom.

Whether writing 'escapist' fiction like *Under the Rose*, which Davies wrote in indifference to 'the bloody public' and entirely '<u>for</u> [him]<u>self</u>', 'embedded' stories of bombs falling on London while poetic souls search for meaning in a crumbling world, or passionate repudiations of the rise of self-obliterating fascism, Davies's response to the war is the development of a 'personal philosophy . . . that nothing on earth can impair one's own interior liberty' (RD to GB 1 July 1940 HRHRC).

11
'Down with passports to art'

In the years following the Second World War, Davies experienced a number of significant changes. The London in which he grew to artistic maturity was gone, taking with it the bookshop that had been the primary institutional pillar of his early career. The slow erosion of Charles Lahr's various socialist bookshops also paralleled both the changing political atmosphere of postwar Britain and Davies's own turning away from Welsh working-class themes. In 1946, the Henley house burnt down and Vincent Wells retired to New Zealand. Then, in the 1950s, Davies's parents died within months of each other. As he explained in a letter to Louis Quinain, 'Now the house there is to be sold, and my last link to the Rhondda is broken. I doubt if I will ever go there again, except to clear up some business, in the near future' (RD to LQ 12 February 1956 NLW MS 23106). In 1956, Davies moved into the Russell Court flat that would be his home until his death.

Given these significant personal political, and geographical shifts, it is not surprising that during and after the Second World War Davies should try to drastically redefine his authorial identity. He does so, primarily, by privileging his identity as an artist over his identity as a Welshman. As we have already seen, this artistic identity is also a reflection of his gay identity, but it was equally deployed in his frequent and persistent denunciations of nationalisms and borders. While these denunciations are couched in humanism and a commitment to the *universal* qualities of art, one gets the strong sense that the only borders Davies really wants to cast off are the Welsh ones that have too closely defined his career. Even as early as 1939, Davies avoided a specifically Welsh definition of himself when he lied to get out of attending a Welsh Literary Luncheon hosted by Foyle's bookshop in which Caradoc Evans, Jack Jones and himself were all to be guests of honour (RD to RM undated NLW MS 20897 E 35). Despite his frequent self-productions as the representative Welshman, Davies cultivated an air of speaking from outside Wales and Welsh life, of having escaped and transcended what he now sees more clearly. His insider's/outsider's gaze, while perfectly tuned to selling a national product to an English audience, reflected his ambivalence regarding his public reception as an Anglo-Welsh author. Accordingly, he frequently advised young Welsh writers to escape the narrow confines of their nationality: 'Live outside of Wales for a time. You will be a better Welshman for it' (Davies, 1943a: 11). Or again: 'Stop thinking of yourself as a Welsh writer. Consort as much as possible with people who dislike Wales. Or, better still, are completely indifferent to her' (quoted. in Baker, 1952: 1).

In 1946, Keidrych Rhys, editor of *Wales*, issued a questionnaire to a number of Anglo-Welsh authors concerning the definition of Anglo-Welsh literature. Davies's responses to some of these questions resist his reduction to the narrow category of 'Anglo-Welsh'. Davies responded to the first question, which read, 'Do you consider yourself an Anglo-Welsh novelist?' (Davies, 1946c: 18), with, 'No. I am only a writer. Does one (if I may make so bold) think of Henry James, T. S. Eliot as Anglo-American writers? Down with passports to Art!' (ibid.). Similarly, when asked, 'Should Anglo-Welsh literature express a Welsh attitude to life and affairs, or should it merely be a literature 'about' Welsh things?' Davies responded,

> Neither consciously. If a writer thinks of his work along these lines it tends to become too parochial, narrow. But if he is Welsh by birth, upbringing, and selects a Welsh background and characters for his work, an essence of Wales should be in the work, giving it a national 'slant' or flavour. But no flag waving. A curse on flag waving. (ibid.)

Four years later, Davies was again brought to task for his representation of Wales in a 1950 BBC radio interview with Glyn Jones.

Jones asks Davies how far he thinks his Wales reflects the *real* Wales. Davies responds by placing the artist's personal prerogative above any commitment to a national subject: 'The "real Wales"? What *is* the real Wales? Whose is it? Is there some final arbiter, is there some absolute opinion of Wales? Surely every genuine writer finds his own Wales' (Jones, 1996: 15). This interview provides Davies's clearest and most high-flown artistic rhetoric. He imagines himself as the very embodiment of artistic expression, explaining,

> I become completely absorbed. I, as a person, am obliterated, my everyday identity is submerged. Personally I think this part of the writer's job is an interesting mystery. As far as I can understand it, I think that when the writer's everyday ego is submerged, the purest part of his mind remains in the ascendant to guide him – or rather, acts as a judge of the mass of raw materials, the dreams and experiences, that are stored in the subconscious. (Jones, 1996: 12)

Davies adapts Freudian language to a Keatsian negative sublime. The true artist has no self and has, therefore, no political commitment or biases – he is the pure servant of his subject. As Davies continues,

> the writer, while writing is in the category of the actor – an actor capable of impersonating anything and anybody, regardless of age, sex, or class. This impersonation or impression certainly can become exhausting, though not for me loathsome. I don't wonder that most good writers I know look worn and somewhat battered, as most actors do off stage. (Jones, 1996: 12)

This 49-year-old Davies, who had by this time enjoyed a decade and a half with Heinemann, has apparently come a long way from anything so crass as an awareness of, let alone a dependence upon, a public and a market. He serves a much higher master now. Indeed, the creative writer 'mustn't write social propaganda or political speeches, [for] his task is to look into the secrets of the eternal private heart' (ibid.: 15).

At the same time that Davies was downplaying his Welshness in the name of art, he was trying to refashion himself in the context of a market that he felt had exhausted Welsh subjects. He was far more aware that he is writing *about* Wales than he lets on to Glyn Jones, for instance, and his idealized claims to artistic transcendence are dubious, to say the least. From at least 1946 onwards, Davies deliberately un-Welshed his fiction and his production under Heinemann. Following the success of *The Black Venus* (1944), Davies wrote to Arnold Gyde, his editor at Heinemann, that he did not 'want to write too much Welsh semi-folk-lore stuff' (RD to AG 9 November 1946 RHAL). Accordingly, although Davies's next novel, *The Dark Daughters* (1947), was partially set in Wales, he stubbornly downplayed the Welsh content. In a synopsis sent to Gyde, Davies explained that while the house in which much of the action occurs is situated in Wales, it

> could be in any country. There is no building of Welsh atmosphere or flavour (except what is intrinsic in the father's character with its blending of mysticism and materialism). My usual Welsh 'inverted' dialogue is not used, since the daughters were born and educated in London and nearly all the other characters are English. (RD AG 9 November 1946 RHAL)

7. Rhys Davies, aged 54.

Heinemann do not seem to have taken Davies very seriously, for, when Davies received the proposed blurb for the novel's jacket, he objected to their emphasis upon the Welsh content of the novel: 'As I have deliberately not played for Welsh background and have attempted to lift the story from particular space and even – fundamentally – time, I would like the word "Welsh" struck out' (RD to AG 17 November 1946 RHAL).

Davies consistently tried to 'strike out' his Welshness, and the next eight novels deliberately avoid the working-class Welsh communities with which his name had become synonymous. For example, *The Painted King* (1954) is loosely based upon the life of Ivor Novello, whose Welsh mother also finds a place in the novel. However, when Davies sends his description of the novel to Gyde for inclusion in Heinemann's Spring List, he insists, 'regarding the mother, I don't want it stated definitely that she is Welsh' (RD to AG 26 October 1953 RHAL). Several years later, when *The Perishable Quality* (1957) is close to publication, Davies strongly objects to Heinemann's dust-jacket. Although this novel, more than any of the other later novels, is set partly in south Wales, most of the action takes place in Carmarthen, bohemian London and an abstracted middle-class home. Again, Davies felt that the novel was only incidentally Welsh. The descriptions of bohemian London illuminate an interesting conflict, for they mean that *The Perishable Quality* represents Davies's overdue engagement with the forms of life that were his primary experience while he wrote almost exclusively about Wales. It is certain that Davies saw this novel as a departure from his earlier writings. So, when confronted with a dust-jacket displaying the gray and narrow streets and looming industrial vista of his youth, he wrote despairingly to A. Dwye Evans that he felt the jacket was inappropriate:

> Many thanks for sending the jacket, but, with one exception, it fills me with dismay. Its very obvious background suggests the very thing I went to great pains to avoid – squalor and a miners' 'cottage' atmosphere. It's true I've dealt with this in the past but it is out of date now and very hackneyed: some of it is in this book – a page or two – but I kept it subdued and marginal and it is of little importance to the book or to the theme

implied in the title. This background is false to the book besides being (for me) artistically repulsive, one of the female faces being especially hideous and badly drawn. (RD to ADE 26 February 1957 RHAL)

Evans did not change the jacket, as he thought it was a good 'selling wrapper' (ADE to RD 1 March 1957 RHAL), and Davies was still being packaged, marketed and sold as Heinemann's Welsh writer.

As press cuttings in the Random House archive and library illustrate, the reviewers of *The Perishable Quality* certainly felt comfortable locating Davies along the lines advertised by the jacket. The *Guardian Journal* praised Davies's 'consummate skill and insight into the character of the Welsh people and towns ... [and the] touch of poetry which is inseparable from the essence of Welshness'. *Time and Tide* claimed that *The Perishable Quality* 'must take its place proudly beside *Tomorrow to Fresh Woods* [and] *The Black Venus*', two of Davies's most Welsh novels, rather than beside the more recent *Dark Daughters* (1947), *Marianne* (1951) or *The Painted King* (1954). Similarly, despite Davies's 'very great pains' to distance himself from his Welsh themes, the *Flint County Herald* tells us that Davies has once again 'given us a lively and shrewd picture of Welsh life'. But by far the best description of Davies's apparently imperishably Welsh quality is this one from *Truth*: 'This is a winner, as tangy as a leek, as fresh as a daffodil, as warm as a knob of Dowlais coal.' Poor Rhys.

While Davies apparently stopped writing of Wales because he felt the subject was out of date, hackneyed and unmarketable, he was unable to escape the perception that he filled a demand for sentimental Welshness from both publishers and reviewers, who felt that he was, in the words of Arnold Gyde, 'more at home in Wales' (AG to RD 3 November 1949 RHAL). However, to be fair to his critics, Davies's new directions in his writing did not stop him from the odd indulgence in the old Welsh flair. *The Perishable Quality* not only lingers in its opening pages in the familiar mining valleys of Davies's earlier novels, but returns to a Carmarthen farm, Penllyn, reminiscent of the one described in *My Wales*, and

8. Front cover of the dust-jacket of *The Perishable Quality* (1957).

includes an account of a poet, Iolo Hancock, easily recognizable as a caricature of Dylan Thomas. *Girl Waiting in the Shade* also retreats into the Welsh countryside, to Henllys, a house 'retaining . . . the original quietude of the scarcely changed vale' (Davies, 1960: 96) where we meet Leyshon, 'a type . . . prevalent around [there]' (ibid.: 114), as 'unspoiled as [the] valley' (ibid.: 106). Even in *The Painted King*, Madame Annie, the mother whom Davies did not want identified definitely as Welsh, wants to take her choir to an 'annual eisteddfod' (Davies, 1954: 94), and hails from 'the countryside where they sing for love . . . Wild moors and valleys of rain [where] the people have this love of singing together' (ibid.: 51). And, to top off Madame Annie's Welshness, her son's theatrical tribute to her life includes 'a concert in melodious Wales' (ibid.: 168). So, there was always some trace of the old Davies in which reviewers could recognize their Welshman.

Davies's consistent fictional returns to Wales were not, however, entirely market driven, for Wales was always part of his personal identity, even if he came to resent it as part of his authorial identity. *The Perishable Quality* is particularly revealing on this point. This novel was published shortly after the death of Davies's parents so, when the central character, Eva, returns to the valley after her bohemian life in London, we perhaps hear some of Davies's own wistfulness: 'She knew it all so well, changed though the valley and the town at its mouth was. She felt she was there in search of a lost identity, of a self that had known happy security' (Davies, 1957: 18). This 'lost identity' was palpable for Davies, who had lost his strongest familial tie to his home and who no longer saw Wales as the primary source of his fictional creativity.

12
Dealing in dark murders

The last phase of Davies's career, from the 1950s to his death in 1978, was mostly concerned with darker social, psychological and sexual themes, coupled with a recurring interest in crime, murder, subterfuge and a sense of ubiquitous surveillance. From the 1950s onward, Davies increasingly wrote fiction that is best described within the generic categories of suburban Gothic and crime fiction. These are perfectly natural vehicles for Davies's new métier. As a queer bachelor, he lived outside and in implicit opposition to traditional domesticity, which was increasingly symbolized by suburban convention and bourgeois self-confinement. As a gay man who, for fifty years, rented rooms in London when being gay was essentially illegal, Davies was intimately aware of living within criminality and under the surveillance of the police.

The first time Davies had tried to 'deal in dark murders', in *Under the Rose*, he felt that he was being told to stay in his place (RD to RM 23 September 1940 NLW MS 20897 E). But, by the 1950s, Davies was increasingly less constricted, both economically and politically, in expressing himself than he had been in 1940. To begin with, he was less constrained by market forces, thanks to several legacies. His parents left most of their estate to him because he had made fewer financial demands on them than did his siblings (Callard, 1994: 69). Next, in 1968, when his close friend Anna Kavan, a writer and heroin addict, finally succeeded in killing herself, Davies again inherited much of her estate (ibid.: 70). Lastly, in the mid-1970s another friend, Louise Taylor, left Davies a legacy of £60, 000 (ibid.: 71). This financial freedom was coupled with political liberation, for Davies's post-Wolfenden Report and post-Stonewall career could now more directly address the authoritative restrictions that had hitherto curtailed any fictional treatment of his identity. In Britain, the 1957 Report of the Departmental Committee on Homosexual Offences and Prostitution led by John Wolfenden recommended the decriminalization of homosexual acts between consenting adults in private. About a decade later, the Stonewall Riots in New York in 1969 sparked an era of open gay rights activism with an almost immediate global influence. These changing political contexts certainly contributed to the fact that Davies's fiction of the 1950s, 1960s and 1970s was often *about* the silence imposed on the first half of his life and career.

Davies was well aware of the interest of the authorities in sexually suggestive fiction. He had been closely involved with Lawrence during the *Lady Chatterley's Lover* affair and had personally smuggled manuscript copies of Lawrence's *Pansies* into Britain so that Charles Lahr could print the first unexpurgated edition. He would also have been intimately aware of James Hanley's run-ins with the Home Office. The homoerotic violence in Hanley's *The German Prisoner* (1930), a limited edition that was also published and printed by Lahr, was banned for obscenity, along with Hanley's second novel, *Boy* (1931), in 1934. Further, Lahr, patron of the arts, counter-cultural publisher and anarchist that he was, followed high-profile censorship cases closely. For example, his personal papers in the Sterling Library include clippings covering both the *Lady Chatterley's Lover* affair and the suppression of Radclyffe Hall's *Well of Loneliness*. Indeed, Davies might even have met Radclyffe Hall at the Cave of Harmony, which he visited while living in a Taviston Street commune in the 1920s. Writing under the surveillance of the censors was an integral component of The Progressive Bookshop coterie. Obviously, therefore, Davies's writing displays a degree of self-policing. Even as late as 1955, Davies's self-edited collection of stories omits all of his gay ones from a list of nearly fifty other titles. As he implies in his preface, his four most queer stories are not among those that yielded their author 'various degrees of satisfaction' but number among those that caused him 'various degrees of unease' (Davies, 1955: vii).

Davies's obsession with surveillance and policing in his later fiction must also have been influenced by fifty years of living as a bachelor in London, a place where queer sexuality was paradoxically enabled and endangered. Gay men were naturally drawn to London by the diverse sociability that the urban metropolis afforded. However, London was also symbolic of economic and imperial power, and 'the queer was a dangerous incursion onto the defining space of Britishness, his presence striking because he seemed so out of place' (Houlbrook, 2005: 24). This alien presence disrupting the 'public' national community resulted in an increased monitoring of queer men and queer spaces. It led, in Matt Houlbrook's words, 'to a culture of knowingness, emphasizing the practical utility of the beat officers' immersion in the realities of metropolitan lowlife, crime and vice' (ibid.: 26). For gay men in London, the figure of the police officer in the public urban space has a particularly charged significance. Indeed, throughout the 1940s and 1950s, corresponding with Davies's growing interest in crime, gay men were subject to more aggressive policing tactics and increasing arrests. Throughout this period, the number of arrests and trials of gay men rose from approximately 200 in 1942 to approximately 650 in 1947. By 1957, the number was still as high as 500 (ibid.: 35). While this trend cannot be applied to all gay men in all London neighbourhoods, it illustrates the general culture of intolerance and surveillance felt by all gay men living in London in the postwar era.

This surveillance did not generally extend into the private sphere, where gay men could depend upon the law's sanctification of domesticity. Nevertheless, the idea of the single gay man troubled and threatened to redefine that domesticity. As an urban bachelor, Davies occupied a particular (though not always visible) category in the psychological landscape of London. The bachelor was an especially destabilizing figure, for he existed on the border of private domesticity and public male independence. As Eve Kosofsky Sedgwick explains, the 'bachelor is at least partly feminized by his attention to and interest in domestic concerns', while 'his intimacy with clubland and bohemia gives him a special

Dealing in dark murders

Figure 9: Rhys Davies examining a male figurine, with a Greek vase in the background.

passport to the world of men as well' (Sedgwick, 1990: 190). In the legal sphere, the bachelor's unfettered movement between a public sphere of male homosociality and a private domestic sphere removed from familial ties rendered him a figure of intense anxiety. Similarly, as Houlbrook explains, courts linked 'the absence of self-control to the residential experience of bachelorhood' (Houlbrook, 2005: 111), assuming that 'a man who lived outside the family could not be expected to conform to social expectations' (ibid.). This bachelorhood was a significant part of Davies's experience. He spent most of his London life living in furnished rooms in those neighbourhoods, such as Maida Vale and Bloomsbury, that catered for single middle-class men, and where a 'complex and distinctive queer world took shape' (ibid.), hidden from the public scrutiny of the police.

That Davies was sensitive to the aberrant reputation of bachelorhood and aware of the anxieties associated with the bachelor's rooms is evident in his fiction. He knew that the bachelor stood opposed to the conventional familial bonds that preserve patriarchal lineal authority. For example, when a defiant son in 'Abraham's Glory' (1942) disregards his prolific father's procreative ambitions, he does so by declaring, 'A bachelor I want to be' (Davies, 1996a: 213). To which his father replies,

> There is no such thing as a bachelor. Live he doesn't. A shadow he is. He folds up early and mopes in death's corner. Death takes him and says: 'Hollow seed this is, no good to the earth, chuck him away'. Into thin air he goes and is not remembered ... Don't you be disgracing me, Gomer. You go out this very evening and set about your true business. There's good and solid young ladies waiting this very minute for what I've given you. (ibid.: 213–14)

In his comic patriarchal zeal, Abraham cannot conceive of anything outside heterosexual procreation, and, therefore, tries to imagine the bachelor out of existence; however, the threat to his heterosexual patriarchal authority is clear.

The bachelor's threat to the stability of domestic order requires active and constant policing, as is evident in Davies's treatment of that quintessential enemy of the bachelor's independence, the English landlady, who stands guard in that anxious liminal space between private and public, the lodging house. In *Print of a Hare's Foot*, Davies's description of the landlady's ubiquitous surveying presence powerfully invokes the experience of living in London during a period of sexual oppression:

> The soulless slatterns of central London ... who let these rooms were of advanced accomplishment in bitchiness. Keyhole spies, they were also gifted with baleful secondsight and the ears of cats. Experts in the bestowal of humiliation, they loured up from the nether regions or a room next to the front door, and, by a single look, could plant cowering guilt in the fresh mind of a country boy or girl. Sometimes, according to their depraved notions, they were justified. (Davies, 1998: 115)

Presiding over a fragmented (usually Victorian) home, often from within the parlour's vestigial domestic sanctity, the landlady stands against the social disintegration of the lodging house. However, this description is particularly significant in its transfer of guilt from the perpetrator accused of a 'crime' to the detector, whose power is predicated upon identifying the 'crime'. It thereby relocates criminality onto policing forces that defend the border between decency and deviance, even if they have to invent a deviance to do so. Essentially, perversity is relocated to the heart of power, and the bachelor, by his mere existence, has revealed that power's artificiality.

Davies claims that his Maida Vale rooms, in which he lived throughout the 1940s and the beginning of the 1950s, were presided over by an exception to his general characterization of landladies. However, even these rooms and the neighbourhood they occupied are remembered within a nexus of sexual libertinism and moral surveillance. Davies recalls in *Print of a Hare's Foot* that prostitutes were 'the bane of Maida Vale' (Davies, 1998: 115), and his landlady refused to have them in the house, because the ground landlords were the Church of England Commissioners, who could withdraw her lease if her house was raided, as so many other houses in the neighbourhood were. Davies's earlier Taviston Street residence, where '[i]n the domain of private morals the quality of mind in a tenant's head counted far more than obedience to English conventions' (ibid.: 117), is also remembered for its connections to sexually permissive London spaces. The commune at 19 Taviston Street hosted several parties that were entertained by Elsa Lanchester and Harold Scott, the founders of the Cave of Harmony, a bohemian nightclub that, as mentioned, welcomed queer habitués like Radclyffe Hall. Similarly, another of Davies's rooms was raided by the police, who believed that he was distributing copies of *Lady Chatterley's Lover*, for he had been corresponding with Lawrence about the arrangements for Lahr's private edition of *Pansies*. Lastly, in a letter to Fred Urquhart, Davies describes a party that fuses the world of the lodging rooms with the queer world of camp and costume balls described, for instance, in 'Wigs, Costumes, Masks' (1949):

> Gascoigne gave a party previous week before going to Vic-Wells ball –
> I was there (not at ball) and got horribly drunk – stupidly drank
> champagne after whiskey (lots). You should have seen the costumes!
> Hughes was in a sort of open-net jumper, with nipples coming through.
> Gascoigne in pink satin breeches and brocaded coat. (RD to FU, no
> date, HRHRC)

As a London lodger, therefore, Davies lived within the psycho-sexual landscapes that operated along embattled borders between the public and the private.

These borders appeared in a specifically queer context in the 1954 novel based on Ivor Novello's experience of closeted celebrity, *The Painted King*. Early in this novel, Davies uses the figure of the landlady to highlight the anxious need to see into the private world of the lodging-house room, which sets the epistemological tone for the subsequent development of the undisclosed queerness at the heart of the public persona of the central character, Guy Aspen. Significantly, the connection between Ivor Novello, bachelorhood, sexual deviance and criminality had been in circulation since Novello's role as the titular lodger in Alfred Hitchcock's 1926 film *The Lodger: A Story of the London Fog*. Michael Williams explains how Novello's public sexual celebrity took an unsettling turn in the role of the ominous bachelor-lodger:

> the mixed feelings of uncertainty, desire and suspicion that greet the pale, mysterious figure of the matinee idol Ivor Novello on the doorstep of the Bloomsbury lodging-house . . . may have been shared by even the most ardent fans who, although familiar with the star in the role of errant lover and Apache hero, had never seen their idol playing the role of a possible serial killer. (Williams, 2003: 42)

The lodger's dangerous bachelorhood incriminates Novello and unsettles his already heavily sexualized public persona with the private depravity behind the 'open secret' of his homosexuality.

A similarly troubling queer confronts the landlady in *The Painted King*. Before the protagonist, Judith, meets Guy, she fails to seduce a young man named Harold. Despite her best efforts, the object of her desire does not respond. Judith wonders at the 'blankness of his face!' (Davies, 1954: 27) and cannot identify the reasons for his lack of interest: 'Had he been magnificently tactful, pretending to be unaware? Or merely shut away in a political ego which vibrated only to public causes, impervious to the sweet needs of private love – yes, yes, it was that' (ibid.: 34). Judith protests too much. She is so desperate to explain Harold's lack of interest that we can be reasonably certain that she has got it wrong.

Our suspicions are confirmed when the moment of revelation arrives, and Harold is discovered by Judith's landlady, Mrs Blow. The name Mrs Blow reappears in *Print of a Hare's Foot* as the woman who catches the childhood Davies stealing fruit from her pear tree, and on whom Davies pees in terror. Barbara Prys-Williams identifies the name of this 'autobiographical' character as a fictional revision, so we may see this childhood experience of fruit-stealing-feminine-terror as subtly linked with the landlady's guilt-bestowing powers of perception. Accordingly, in *The Painted King*, Harold stands for the landlady's knowledge and the reader's ignorance. Judith 'had not yet learned that all landladies possess second sight' (ibid.: 28), so as she and Harold attempt to sneak past Mrs Blow's door, the landlady bursts onto the landing declaring, 'I *thought* so!' (ibid.). After Harold leaves, Judith tearfully exclaims, 'It's not true! It's not true!' (ibid.). We are not explicitly told what 'it' is, but Mrs Blow, in her absolute surveying knowledge, needs no telling:

> 'What!' she exclaimed, and gave her lodger another close, all-embracing look.
>
> 'It's not true.'
>
> 'My God,' whispered Mrs. Blow. 'The big tyke! I believe you're speaking the truth . . . My God,' she remarked as her lodger, shatteringly disorganized, crept into the cosy parlour, 'a big, strapping fellow like him . . . All the same,' she warned, 'I won't have them going in and going out; let this be a warning to you.' (ibid.: 28–9)

In this scene, we see a knowing that tries not to know (in part by never explicitly naming) a disruptive sexual difference, followed by a retreat into the all-seeing landlady's 'cosy parlour'. As contemporary queer theory has demonstrated, maintaining heteronormative patriarchal hegemony requires this simultaneous knowing and unknowing of homosexual practice. It must invoke difference to define itself against it, and then suppress the knowledge of that difference in order to maintain the illusion of an unchallenged and homogenous normality. This process is what led Foucault to claim that sex is 'ostentatiously' hidden or silenced 'by formulating the matter in the most explicit terms' (Foucault, 1990: 9).

This is why police are such interesting figures in Davies's fiction, generally, and in his later crime fiction, more specifically. They are the physical embodiment of law and order, a symbol of the serene safety of modern civil society. Yet, like the landladies who 'plant guilt in fresh minds', they inevitably imply the criminality against which they stand. In order to 'put away' criminals, the police must shine their flashlights into dark corners to reveal, know and name 'abnormal' or 'evil' behaviours. On the surface, this public knowing and naming establishes clear boundaries between the 'proper' and the 'perverse'. Beneath the surface, it reveals that the 'proper' and the 'perverse' are mutually defining terms that depend upon one another. As we saw with Davies's playfulness with militarism and uniforms, Davies delights in this ambiguity on the thresholds of authority and criminality. According to Fred Urquhart, with whom Davies shared a cottage in Tring in the summer of 1946, Davies had a sexual obsession with guardsmen (Callard, 1991: 68), a desire that is founded in the interstices of power and pleasure. This desire is also playfully illustrated in 'Wigs, Costumes, Masks' (1949) when Mr Simon offers to transform the two investigating policemen into 'magnificently barbaric Royal Guards of Queen Catherine' (Davies, 1996c: 376). Their faces, he tells them, 'would become so Russian that [their] own wives wouldn't recognize [them], and just think what refreshing escapades that might lead to!' (ibid.). This shiftiness between policing and criminality is also seen in the close family relationship between the literary bachelor and the literary private detective, both operating from their urban bachelor pads. The detective is a flâneur, a detached urban watcher, and he is dangerously close to the forms of criminality that he observes. As Scott McCracken explains, the detective in this sense 'facilitates a transgressive act, [and] ... it is a matter of debate whether the narrative of detection confirms or disrupts the social boundaries transgressed' (McCracken, 1998: 63).

Given Davies's career of repressing his queer subject-matter in his fiction, and given his fifty years of living as a gay bachelor under the punitive surveillance of the London authorities, we should not be surprised to find that crime and police feature very strongly in Davies's fiction throughout the 1950s, 1960s and 1970s. So prevalent is crime that the final stage of Davies's career is usefully approached through the lens of crime fiction, as opposed to classic detective fiction.

The police in classic detective fiction stand for more general matrices of knowledge and power. For example, writing about the nineteenth-century detective novel, D. A. Miller explains that

> the limits of the detective's knowledge become the limits of his power as well: his astonishing explications double for a control exercised in the interests of law and order. Detective fiction is thus always implicitly punning on the detective's brilliant super-vision and the police super-vision that it embodies. His intervention marks an explicit bringing-under-surveillance of the entire world of the narrative. (Miller, 1988: 35)

So, 'when Sherlock Holmes deduces a man's moral and economic history from his hat in "The Adventure of the Blue Carbuncle"' (ibid.) he opens up 'the fearful prospect of an absolute surveillance under which everything would be known, incriminated, policed' (ibid.). Davies's crime fiction acknowledges and seeks to evade this rationalist, all-knowing 'detecting' presence through a more noirish 'gothic representation of excess, violence and transgressions of the boundaries of reason and law' (Horsley, 2005: 4).

Although Davies wrote crime fiction as early as 1940 in *Under the Rose*, he claimed in 1945 that he was 'ignorant of thrillers, detectives, murder stories etc.' (RD to LQ 7 February 1945 NLW MS 23106 E).

However, he wrote this denial to a friend, Louis Quinain (who also happened to be a country policeman), just before recommending Vera Caspary's *Laura*, the 1942 noir thriller that, in 1944, was made into a film that helped give birth to the film noir genre. Noir is 'characterized by its stress on the subjective point of view, by the shifting roles of the protagonist, and by the ill-fated relationship between the protagonist and society, generating the themes of alienation and entrapment' (Horsley, 2005: 115). The protagonists of noir 'can be victims, transgressors, or investigators. They cannot, however, be the confident, all-solving investigators we have encountered in classic detective fiction' (ibid.: 116), and noir plots 'turn on falsehoods, contradictions, and misrepresentations, and the extent to which all discourse is flawed and duplicitous is a dominant theme' (ibid.). Noir fiction belongs to the more general category of crime fiction, which tends to focus on the psychology of the criminal rather than the detective, though the detective is usually present in a secondary role. Finally, like noir, crime fiction tends to question law and society (Scaggs, 2005: 107–8). These definitions apply very nicely to much of Davies's later fiction.

Laura is a fascinating read in its own right, but offers particular interest when read in light of Davies's fiction. Set in New York, this story of murder and mistaken identity is told from three perspectives. The first part of the story is told by Waldo Lydecker, a writer, art collector and aesthete queer bachelor; the second part is told by Marc McPherson, a typical noir detective presenting a hard-boiled exterior that masks a shaken masculinity; and the third part is told by Laura Hunt, an independent and successful advertising agent who refuses to be owned by any man. Briefly, the story begins when Laura's body is discovered in her apartment with her face blown off by a shotgun blast. In the course of the investigation, Detective McPherson falls in love with the victim. When Laura reappears in the apartment, presumably unaware that she has been pronounced dead, McPherson must face the unpleasant fact that Laura might have murdered the deceased girl, who was in fact a model engaged in an affair with Laura's fiancé, Shelby Carpenter. Ultimately, however, Waldo Lydecker is revealed as the true murderer. With the collector's obsessive need to preserve sole ownership of his protégé, he would rather kill her than let her marry Shelby.

Lydecker's criminality is clearly connected with his queered bachelorhood. His dandified bachelor's rooms betray a feminized domestic flair; in particular, his obsessive collecting of porcelain, art and glassware is not only explicitly linked to Freudian anal eroticism, but is a trait that renders him a natural subject of investigative surveillance. For example, McPherson studies Lydecker and wonders,

> What made a man collect old glassware and china? Why did he carry a stick and wear a beard? What caused him to scream when someone tried to drink out of his pet coffee cup? Clues to character are the only clues that add up to the solution of any but the crudest crime. (Caspary, 1957: 206)

Based upon misrecognition, the crude and brutal murder at the heart of the novel becomes abstracted into a figurative violence against Laura. This abstracted, subtler, less tangible and less nameable criminality circulates within Lydecker's enigmatic character. These more subtle forms of criminality and detection are consistent with Davies's fiction and are announced early in *Laura*, as Lydecker ruminates on the generic limitations of the mystery novels:

> I still consider the conventional mystery story as an excess of sound and fury, signifying, far worse than nothing, a barbaric need for violence and revenge in that timid horde known as the reading public. The literature of murder investigation bores me as profoundly as its practice irritated Mark McPherson. Yet I am bound to tell this story, just as he was obliged to continue his searches out of a deep emotional involvement in the case of Laura Hunt. I offer the narrative, not so much as a detective yarn as a love story. (ibid.: 20)

Laura opposes rationalist detective fiction and is less concerned with an omniscient meting out of retribution than with the social and psychological ambiguities of postwar identities. With its shifting narration, its unstable masculinity, its threatening femininity and its examination of alienated deviance, *Laura* is prototypically noir. When one thinks of such novels as *Under the Rose* (1940), *Marianne* (1951), *Nobody Answered the Bell* (1971) and *Ram with Red Horns* (1996), all of which focus on the psychology of murdering women in vaguely Gothic domestic settings, it is not hard to understand Davies in these terms. It is, therefore, appropriate that Davies won the Edgar Award, America's highest honour for crime writers, for his 1966 short story, 'The Chosen One'. The story is set in Wales and concerns a wealthy landowning woman who, equipped with powerful binoculars, surveys her tenant, whom she ultimately manipulates into carrying out her own murder.

Davies specifically undermines the nineteenth-century rationalist detective in two obviously (though not explicitly) queer stories set in the surveillance-ridden context of London: the early short story 'The Romantic Policewoman' (1931) and a later story, 'Wigs, Costumes, Masks' (1949). In 'The Romantic Policewoman', the policewoman's rational efforts to police and redeem a fallen woman mask her unwillingness to know and name her lesbianism, thereby straining the boundaries she seeks to defend. The story revolves around a policewoman, Ella Dobson, who rescues a young unemployed working girl, Kathleen, from the streets and a life of prostitution. Ella's professional duties as a policewoman signal her entrapment within the very authority that she represents. She is an instance of what Eva in *The Perishable Quality* describes as 'the police we all carry about with us' (Davies, 1957: 16). She is *self-policing*, and her own desires are in conflict with her authoritarian, prescriptive role as the representative of the 'rules and regulations' (Davies, 1996c: 200, 206) that prohibit homosexuality: 'She was doing useful, even noble work. Yet . . . yet it was so impersonal: rules and regulations were such cold dead things' (ibid.: 200). Ella claims that she is 'a policewoman, but [she has] a soul of [her] own too' (ibid.: 205), one she tries to reveal by offering Kathleen a striptease, which the girl watches, transfixed by the performative display:

> 'I must get this uniform off,' said Ella, entirely the chatty woman now. 'It's that stiff and heavy, it'll be a relief to get into something soft.'

> Kathleen followed every movement, staring at each piece as it was removed – the business-like belt, the ominous whistle and chain, the great tunic and greater skirt, the tall strong boots. But there was no truncheon and no pair of handcuffs visible. Then the girl's eyes became rounder as she saw the delicate rose and pink silk of the policewoman's underthings. (ibid.: 204)

Ella makes a spectacle of dismantling the 'pieces' of a 'stiff and heavy' identity that does not comprise the whole of herself. She performs the unmaking of herself, and she emerges from beneath the 'ominous' whistle, which suggests exposure, and chain, which suggests captivity. Interestingly, the more obviously violent and restrictive signs of her authority are not necessarily absent, but only 'not visible', indicating the more pernicious (because unseen) forms of control restraining Ella.

The reader must be an investigative one to discern Ella's motives, and it is no coincidence that Ella is an investigative figure who challenges us by her inability to investigate herself. When Kathleen abruptly leaves, Ella begins to search for her, and a 'scheme of detective work [forms] in her mind' (ibid.: 209). Imagining that she is on a mission to save Kathleen from the cruel masculine world, she tracks the girl to her former lover. When Ella tries to liberate Kathleen, Kathleen's lover grows angry and reveals the truth of Ella's motives. But the text of the story never explicitly states Ella's implied lesbianism and so never completely releases the repressed truth that carries the narrative, and we are left in a kind of un-knowing knowledge:

> 'God Almighty, I've had enough of this,' he snarled. 'Policewoman or no, I'll let you know what I know –'. He lowered his face, alive with a derisive contempt, and began to hiss almost into Ella's mouth words that turned her to stone. Kathleen shrunk back, white and helpless. He finished with an epithet that turned Ella's blood cold with a fear new to her. Then he lifted his shoulders, flashed her a look of warning, and stretched his arm protectively to Kathleen. They left the café.
> She sat gazing before her as if stricken. For some moments there prowled in her eyes the terror of revelation. (ibid.: 213)

Ella now knows what Kathleen's lover knows, but can we be sure that *we* know? What has been revealed that is so terrifying to this representative of rules, regulations and the authorities that monitor and safeguard the moral order? 'The Romantic Policewoman' is a narrative act of silenced knowledge whose revelation is hidden within the story's logic of repression. More importantly, Davies again inverts the policing authority to reveal the 'perversity' at the heart of the power, and to illustrate that efforts to know and name 'deviance' are efforts to impose boundaries where none in fact exist.

These boundaries are fully and finally obliterated in 'Wigs, Costumes, Masks', which also undermines the authorities that seek to monitor and maintain the boundary between the 'proper' and the 'perverse'. The story begins with the two rational detectives, Frank and Jimmy, standing in the shadows while carefully surveying a shop in 'a district devoted to the night entertainment of the flesh' (Davies, 1996c: 372). They are interested in Mr Simon, a costume dealer whom they suspect of some undisclosed crime, but who will ultimately elude their gaze through a fantastic display of theatrical illusion that obliterates their rational fact-finding inquiry. The story particularly emphasizes the relationship between seeing, knowing and policing. When Frank and Jimmy interview Mr Simon, who is dressed grandly as a rajah, they insist that they have 'come looking for facts' (ibid.: 376). This faith in straightforward empirical knowledge is immediately stressed by descriptions of Frank 'looking from under his lids' (ibid.), and Jimmy whose 'eyes [are] still observing in that non-observant way of his profession' (ibid.). As they interrogate Mr Simon, 'bright with concentrated search, the two pairs of eyes became ranged full on the rajah' (ibid.). Mr Simon, however, challenges the interrogative fact-finding eyes with an altogether different eye:

> 'Facts!' continued the rajah, in the silence. 'What are facts?' Pointing to the nude wax-headed figure, to the casket of jewellery, to the raven-black page-boy's wig, he asked: 'Would these be called facts? For me, yes. Reliable facts. The same as a glass eye is more of a fact than a real eye: it lasts, gentlemen.' (ibid.)

Davies exploits that aesthete's privileging of art over nature, much as he did in 'Cherry-Blossom on the Rhine', dismissing objective 'truth' as a lie preserved to rob life of its true complexity and subtlety. The wax figures and costumes in Mr Simon's shop 'testified to the truth that art can always set nature's deficiencies at naught' (ibid.), echoing Vivian's claim in Oscar Wilde's *Decay of Lying* that 'What art really reveals to us is nature's lack of design, her curious crudities, her extraordinary monotony, her absolute unfinished condition' (Wilde, 2002: 1858). This posture blurs the division between natural and unnatural, replacing the notion of biologically fixed bodies with more fluid performances of sexual and gender identities.

For Mr Simon is a 'liberating magician' (Davies, 1996c: 381) who, like Guy Aspen in *The Painted King*, does 'not belong to the precise realism of the day and always there [is] about him a hint of the pantomime kingdom' (ibid.: 375). He helps people 'become for an illicit night the creatures of their dreams, [who] spread an atmosphere of enchanted liberation as they [flee] through shafts of changing tints' (ibid.: 381). His world of revelry and transformation obliterates the borders of time and space, fantasy and reality, and it threatens, even as the detectives enter his shop, to transform the solid world of facts into one of excessive possibility:

> Queen Elizabeth sat there on a throne, dressed to receive at least the French Ambassador, her handsome brocades and ropes of pearls perhaps too garish, the pointed face, and even the little hands, too rigidly shrewish. A Blackamoor arrayed in scarlet and Prussian blue grinned impudently at the two men while, perched over him, a huge extravagantly-coloured parrot watched them in petrified silence. Everlastingly smiling, a Chinaman stood with hands inside the sleeves of a pretty kimono, quite at home with his companion, a high-wigged Western lady in a lilac crinoline, who peeped over her fan at the intruders. But most splendid of all was the Fairy Queen whose butterfly wings had carried her, in her rose-tulip bodice, pale green gossamer skirt and star-lit shoes, to a dais for their inspection; charmingly, she wanted also to touch their raincoated shoulders with her silver blue wand. Withdrawn into the background other presences watched; a Roundhead, a Puritan, a Jack-of-Spades, a monk, a Plantagenet king. (ibid.: 373)

This world is 'extravagant' in the truest sense of the word, which denotes a wandering out of bounds, for there are no national, racial or temporal borders separating these figures of history, fairy tale and legend, who 'impudently' 'watch' and 'peep' back at the investigators. And the Fairy Queen, whose name is composed of two slang words for homosexual men, longs for the magical transformation of the detectives, a feat achieved when Frank and Jimmy must dress up to pursue Mr Simon to the costume ball.

Despite their efforts, the detectives fail to draw Mr Simon into their world of facts. First, he withdraws into an inner room and replaces himself with a wax replica dressed 'in his rusty black jacket and stiffly formal if soiled white collar and cuffs' (ibid.: 379) with 'red wool socks' on his feet (ibid.). His businessman-like appearance is reinforced by his concentration on documents on the desk and a room decked out in conventional middle-class masculinity: 'The room was heavily furnished in a middle-class Victorian style, solid with mahogany sideboard, enormous vases, a sofa, basket chairs, oil-paintings of cattle and shaggy dogs' (ibid.). The whole illusion, apart from the red socks, suggests the sloughed-off husk of a conventional and readily recognizable masculine self, which both detectives naturally believe on sight.

Failing to catch Mr Simon at the ball, the detectives return to the shop. While watching from outside, they observe someone within setting fire to the rooms. As the fire grows, they wait for Mr Simon to emerge, but he never does. The figure that falls from the upper-storey window, 'Down to the solidity, the malevolent facts, the punishment below' (ibid.: 388), wears a conspicuous 'long sock of warm red wool on the shoeless foot' (ibid.). The true Mr Simon simply disappears into the magical conflagration, that resists the firemen who arrive, 'factual in steel and thick tunics' (ibid.: 387). The mercurial fire offers a last resistance to the detectives when it appears in the vague form of a 'doll-like creature' (ibid.) that could be Mr Simon or the Fairy Queen, but which is in fact all and any of the myriad shapes:

> Even as the group looked at this mystic figure-piece, an unknown native of the flames, it exploded into hyacinthine glory, self-consuming, a

phoenix death, a bursting figure crested with curly feathers of reddish-purple and footed about with swarming dragon-tongues eyed like the tails of peacocks: it gave a last flare of violet, gold and rose, and vanished into ashen smoke. (ibid.)

This many-eyed figure of transformation and transcendence offers a consolation to the more common and factual 'punishment' of Mr Simon's doppelgänger. The suicidal leap of the besieged and harried Mr Simon undoes the experience of death and failure that too often characterizes the queer narrative. In its place we have this last vanishing trick of the 'liberating magician' (ibid.: 381).

No such liberation is achieved in Davies's 1971 novel *Nobody Answered the Bell*, in which Davies explicitly links closeted homosexuality with hidden criminal guilt. The novel begins with Kenny rushing to help her lesbian lover Rose, who has just violently murdered her stepmother, Georgette. On her way to aid Rose, even before she learns of the crime, she passes a 'policeman with a flashlamp examin[ing] shadowy doorways' (Davies, 1971: 9), reminding us of the surveillance probing into secret places. Not coincidentally, the stepmother was the only person who knew of Rose and Kenny's love, and she possessed a 'deadly knowledge' (ibid.: 19). Kenny and Rose hide the body in a cupboard in the attic and engage in an elaborate scheme to cover up their crime. Dressing Kenny in Georgette's clothing, they play-act the stepmother's departure to Hull, creating viable evidence for inquisitive neighbours and police.

Thereafter, they live in conventional domestic peace in Rose's house, ignoring the rotting corpse above them, and cutting themselves off from the rest of the world more and more. Kenny seeks most zealously to domesticate and normalize the relationship, becoming more obviously masculine in tweeds and cap, and even purchasing a strap-on penis for aggressive lovemaking with her delicate Rose. However, their efforts at normality are dogged by the dead woman in the attic, the 'deadly knowledge' corrupting their love. The more obvious crime of murder, literally closeted and unmentioned, stands for the criminality of their relationship, the guilt and shame eroding their efforts to blend into the suburban normality of the neighbourhood. Their relationship quickly degenerates into a series of lies, cheating, deception and surveillance of each other.

The self-destructive secrecy of their love comes to a head when Kenny secretly removes Georgette's body from the attic and buries it in the front garden. She tries to defend herself, but only reveals the terrible burden of their criminal desire:

> 'God knows who might turn up yet, asking questions.' Beyond the staircase landing, she switched on another light. Then she ran and dodged past the crook-backed white figure; confronting it, she entreated, in a less distraught voice, 'Listen! We must stay together quietly, we must, we must!' (ibid.: 150)

Rose, physically rotting with a degenerative bone disease, has faded into a crooked wraith, while Kenny tries desperately to dispel the darkness, switching on lights even as she begs for a further retreat into their protective silence. That night, while Kenny sleeps, Rose delivers three firm blows with a hammer to Kenny's head, then strangles her. Finally, Rose too dies, while trying to hide Kenny in the attic cupboard.

This suburban Gothic crime novel exposes the surveying authorities trapping gay men and lesbians in a silence that amounts to death. In it, we see a culmination of Davies's use of crime and murder to explore dark passions and criminal desires. Forms of policing and surveillance were central to Davies's life as a gay man in London and are evident throughout his career, becoming ever more evident following his first foray into crime fiction in *Under the Rose*. Davies was certainly concerned with the policing of sexuality in the early 1930s in such stories as 'The Romantic Policewoman', which we have already discussed, and 'Doris of Gomorrah', which depicts a young girl's naive encounter with the sexual variety within London's Bohemia and respectable middle-class domesticity. Nevertheless, by the 1950s much more of Davies's work deals implicitly with his own closeted sexuality.

13
A 'borderline case'

Davies's last novel published in his lifetime, *Honeysuckle Girl* (1975), was loosely based on the life of his friend, Anna Kavan. It does not revolve around murder, but it demonstrates a similarly criminalized removal from normative life in defiance of the authoritative structures that seek to monitor and control. Specifically, *Honeysuckle Girl* uses drug addiction as a metaphor for a more general desire to step out from under the surveillance of the normative patterns of life. In this novel, the policing authorities of Davies's previous work are augmented by medical authorities, who also seek to name, define and guard borders. It explores what Kavan described in 1948 as 'the struggle of those who try to make themselves a home on a homeless borderland' (quoted in Callard, 1992: 61). Ultimately, this novel eradicates these borders through a final retreat into the unfettered self towards which Davies had striven for most of his career.

Karen, the central character of *Honeysuckle Girl*, is a singularly detached figure. Her father is a ghostly non-presence who committed suicide before Karen could know him, and her mother is a wealthy provider of financial support and emotional indifference who spends her life travelling around the world, alighting briefly in Karen's life for obligatory visits. When the novel begins, Karen is in a loveless and sexless marriage and has just recovered from an operation for the removal of an ovarian cyst following a miscarriage.

All familial and emotional ties are either severed or severely attenuated, yet, echoing the setting of *Nobody Answered the Bell*, in the early pages of the novel, Karen is found in the sturdy domesticity of a London suburb, sitting 'in the pretty garden of a firmly rooted English country house' (Davies, 1975: 1). In fact, all three of Davies's last novels, *Nobody Answered the Bell*, *Honeysuckle Girl* and *Ram with Red Horns*, deal with criminal women in conflict with their domestic spaces, which had always been closely related to Davies's need to redefine domesticity and the idea of home in order to reconcile his private selfhood with the various public definitions of 'home'. Karen's sitting room has 'a look of country repose' (ibid.: 3) with its 'plumpy luxurious sofa' (ibid.) and 'matching chairs of equally stuffy bulk' (ibid.), at which Karen stares 'as if one day, in an access of systematic destruction, she would rip a dagger into the brocade and disembowel the bloated but expensive monsters' (ibid.). Rather than providing a sense of home and belonging, the 'black-beamed sitting room' is a cage of enforced inactivity where 'all life seemed to be tucked away in the abeyance of interior domestic security' (ibid.: 18).

Karen's distance from the world of domestic propriety is partly defined in relation to art, for she is also the last of Davies's defiant visionary artists. Unlike her husband's abstract paintings, she exercises a 'serene academic style . . . in glowingly alive brush-strokes' (ibid.: 3), with 'no hint of discordance or inner tumult' (ibid.: 8). Like Davies, who claimed to be so 'completely absorbed' in his writing that he 'as a person, [was] obliterated, [his] everyday identity . . . submerged' (Jones, 1996: 12), Karen too became 'so utterly absorbed in a painting that she seemed herself the brush, the paper or canvas, herself the subject, the unhesitant colours' (Davies, 1975: 63). Her husband wonders if this absorption is why 'all her work, however trite the subject and conventional the treatment, carried a living entity, touchable, breathing, communicating readily with the viewer' (ibid.). Significantly, Karen and her husband do not communicate, and in fact, her art is largely an effort to impose structure on an exterior world from which she is detached:

> She loved trees, flowers, animals, birds, with a kind of pure escape into the precision of their growth, movement, their pattern of corporeal existence, their meaning to the eye; the consequent pantheistic satisfaction

lying beyond this could bring equilibrium to her being. That was why her paintings were so serene; they were therapeutic. So far, she had not attempted human subjects, perhaps because they demanded more than she could provide in identification. (ibid.: 6)

Karen, then, perfectly fits the formula of the visionary artist who, like the rest of Davies's deviants and outcasts, communicates from a reality removed from the world in which most people move.

When Karen first attempts to escape her domestic prison not just through art, but in body as well, she drives to London, where she meets Chris in the train station. Chris is the last of Davies's queer bachelors. In this final novel, however, Davies revises the bachelor/landlady conflict by making Chris the proprietor and master of the home, thereby introducing a more positively mercurial experience of bachelor freedom. In Chris's company, Karen realizes her need to 'retreat from the pattern by which the so-called "comfortable" lived' (ibid.: 29), but on departure from his house, she is immediately confronted by a policeman who 'surveyed her with a subtle suspicion, both non-committal and accusing' (ibid.: 32). Karen wonders if Chris's house, like Mr Simon's, is 'under observation, its owner's nocturnal perambulations known' (ibid.), and she defensively strikes the policeman. Not responding to the violence, he informs Karen that he had been 'keeping an eye' (ibid.: 33) on her. His surveillance probably derives from a belief that she does not belong to this London of 'nocturnal perambulations', where gay men like her mother's assistant, Dick Haines, may find 'free nights for experienced forages among the small West End clubs catering to his minority tastes' (ibid.: 49). The policeman, therefore, takes Karen into custody until her husband can pick her up and return her to her proper domestic restfulness.

However, Karen's drug addiction and depression continually disrupt her 'country repose'. When Karen's addiction to heroin is discovered, she is sent to a withdrawal clinic, and, when she later attempts suicide, she is committed to a psychiatric clinic. The medical control to which Karen is subjected is an insidious one that masquerades as a benevolent curative aid. For example, the withdrawal clinic is 'strict, yet curiously friendly in a kind of rational way. No assertion of accusations, no lecturing; and no molestation from the affliction of love, no references to sexual matters' (ibid.: 67). Although she is eventually given a key to the 'tall iron gates, set in a wall fringed thickly with trees', Karen knows that she is 'still under surveillance' (ibid.: 81). Significantly, the same benevolent medical authority appears in Davies's early short story, 'The Doctor's Wife' (1930), where, like the policemen in 'Wigs, Costumes, Masks', it figures in direct relation to the failure of hegemonic sexual knowledge to know and, therefore, control homosexuality.

Specifically, 'The Doctor's Wife' depicts the resilient ignorance of hetero-normativity through the obstreperously masculine heterosexual doctor's inability to recognize his wife's lesbian affair. The titular doctor, Dr Morgan, stands for an institution that had always sought to identify and 'cure' sexual deviance, the results of which Davies viewed unfavourably. As he reports in *Print of a Hare's Foot*, the one man he knew who tried to have his homosexuality 'cured' through psychoanalysis and glandular injections was only made ill: 'Previously a normal talker, and of equitable temperament, he developed a bad stammer and twitched like a marionette' (Davies, 1997: 106). As Davies's language suggests, the treatment was the aberration, disrupting the man's previously 'normal' state. Further, comparing the man to a marionette reminds us that his behaviour is governed by some greater controlling hand. Similarly, in *Honeysuckle Girl*, Karen's mother reports with a Lady Bracknell-like unconcern that she 'believes [psychologists] can be miraculous. A married friend of mine . . . had a course with one in New York and became so placid that she and her husband ended up looking at television for hours every night' (Davies, 1975: 54).

Not surprisingly, therefore, Dr Morgan's description dominates the opening of 'The Doctor's Wife'. We learn that he has a 'pleasantly bullying way' (ibid.) and a 'rough didactic manner' (ibid.). The valley feels it is 'nice to have such a large influential looking man bothering in such a masterful way about them' (ibid.). Dr Morgan is an earlier instance of the doctor in the clinic where

Karen must have her prescription filled. This later smiling doctor is 'a countryside man with a golfer's or cricketer's air' (Davies, 1975: 153), with 'a faint touch of deference, behind an authoritarian power lying compact and absolute in his breezy haleness' (ibid.). Also, in league as he is with the policing authorities of the novel, 'his iron blue eyes . . . were adroit in their sorting out of truth from lies' (ibid.). Dr Morgan's influence also reaches beyond the strictly medical authority over bodies, for he exercises power in the political sphere as well:

> He took an interest in the local governing bodies, too, and had his way in no uncertain fashion; people said he would go to Westminster in the end. There was scarcely a political or local council meeting that did not contain his large fighter's head, but he said things in such a magnetic way, with jokes stuck here and there, that no one could resist him. (Davies, 1996c: 137)

The double meaning of 'governing bodies' stresses the pervasive reach of medical authority. Indeed, Dr Morgan is also the presumptive master of his dreamy harp-playing wife's frail health, and he intends to improve her physically as well as socially. He informs her, 'Now, Phoebe . . . you're going to be a new woman. I shall take you to pieces and build you up again. A doctor's wife must be an example to the place' (ibid.: 138).

Unfortunately for Dr Morgan, his governing of bodies does not truly extend to his wife's body, for he is 'still waiting for her' (ibid.: 139), and Phoebe increasingly prefers the company of Agnes Wright, 'a sturdy, handsome woman with strong cheeks, clear pale-blue eyes and good vigorous limbs' (ibid.).

The doctor's presumed authority quickly becomes ridiculous because it operates within a world that his wife has rejected. Phoebe, like Karen and Mr Simon (and like Guy Aspen and Owen Llewellyn), is 'one of those people who seem to live in a different world from our ordinary coarse workaday one' (ibid.: 140). So complete is the epistemological absence of homosexuality in this story that even when the doctor, intent on catching his wife with her lover, surprises the couple kissing in Agnes's home, he is blind to the truth:

> He drew back and went slowly and softly to the door. His head hung down a bit sheepishly. He felt he had intruded on something rather beautiful where he had no business. He realized the close friendship that existed between Agnes and Phoebe. It was nice and unusual to see two women so fond of each other. And he admired Agnes as a fine social worker, in spite of her over-shadowing of Phoebe's personality. He had seen them, through the chink, kissing each other in such a sweet way. He felt ashamed. He would, however, go in, he would be very nice to them. He would forget his suspicions for a moment. (ibid.: 144)

This moment of revelation is lost on the doctor and, perhaps, on one or two readers as well. The closest he comes to realization is the dim feeling that arises when speaking to Agnes of his appreciation for the friendship between her and his wife:

> The pale gleam behind Agnes's eyes became brighter as she looked into the Doctor's eyes. Her strong handsome face was lifted up close to his and he thought there was something queer about her expression, a flash of something that repelled him for the moment. (ibid.: 139)

Nor is this relationship the only sign of a queer world operating under the noses of this respectable middle-class south Wales community. Of all the men the doctor suspects of sleeping with his wife, he chooses Emlyn Walters, a poet and actor with a 'flippant voice' (ibid.: 143), 'delicate feminine features and hair longer than a man's should be. He wore a scarlet tie and a big Egyptian ring' (ibid.). Although Dr Morgan thinks that this artistic dandy 'looked and behaved . . . like a nancy-boy' (ibid.: 144), looking and behaving never materialize into *being*. When he finally confronts Phoebe and Emlyn, suggestively growling, 'You look a pretty couple there' (ibid.: 145), Phoebe bursts out laughing.

So hopeless is this cuckold that one cannot sympathize with him as a victim of infidelity. One feels, rather, relief for Phoebe, Agnes and Emlyn, all of whom, much as Davies did, escape to the artistic and theatrical freedoms of London. Right up to the end of the story, the doctor demonstrates a power made impotent because it is exercised in vain over a world whose dynamics he cannot perceive. He writes possessive letters beginning 'My Own Darling' (ibid.: 149) and signed 'Your husband' (ibid.), and he asks whether or not Phoebe has fallen in love with another man, ending his letter, as the story ends, by 'adding masterfully, "But I warn you I'd thrash his life out if only I could lay my hands on him!"' (ibid.). The irony of these last words, like the irony of the story's title, is that there is nothing this domineering doctor can *lay his hands on*. This man whose profession involves handling and curing bodies cannot grasp desires outside the normative code upon which his authority is predicated; therefore, the entire institutional framework that the doctor represents becomes laughably powerless.

Karen is equally 'incurable'. Deciding that she is a 'borderline case', she gives in to her dreamlike existence in the Swiss psychiatric clinic. Her detachment eludes the luxurious clinic's designs upon her, even though, as she explains to her fellow-inmate Erich, 'The gates are locked. The walls are high' (Davies, 1975: 100). Indeed, Karen's captivity in the asylum is part of her realization of escape from the normative world and its need to draw distinctions and create limits. She therefore transforms restriction into release and possibility. Accordingly, when Erich asks Karen if a patient who had tried to escape had his passport with him, Karen tells him, 'We do not have passports here – no right to them' (ibid.: 103). They have no right to passports because they do not acknowledge the reality of the invisible borders that the rest of the world accepts through mutual consent, just as Davies proclaimed that there are no passports to art, and just as he mocks the antics of border guards. And from Erich, Karen learns of Helmut, who is loosely based on Charles Lahr and his stateless existence, and with whom Karen shares her life upon release from the clinic. As Erich and Karen sit in Karen's room under the watchful presence of 'an eye in the peep-hole' (ibid.: 115) belonging to Nurse Renata (retina?), Erich explains that Helmut, having refused British naturalization, is 'without a country', '[a]lways a refugee' and 'belongs nowhere' (ibid.: 114–15). This is the country into which Laura finally moves.

By the end of the novel, Karen, too, belongs nowhere, and her suicide is figured as the only escape for those who cannot live within the rigid boundaries of identification offered by normative society. In the final pages of the novel, Karen returns to the secluded riverside grove where she used to find release from her domestic prison. On this site, she used to meet the lesbian nurse whose penetrative heroin injections relieved an erotic yearning for Karen's soft skin, and here Karen yielded to adulterous lovemaking with a young visiting male cousin. Karen climbs 'a five-barred, chain-locked gate' (ibid.: 163), arrives at the river, administers a massive overdose of heroin and patiently waits to die:

> She lay flat on her stomach, her head over the verge of the bank, looking into silvered water, a mirror, alive in a clear glinting. She looked down into her own face lying below the glassy surface of water, entangled there among idly swaying lily-stems, and the cool water flowed along her healed limbs, and the image was transmuted into an organic identity truly here at last, not to be dissolved. (ibid. 165)

As Karen lies 'on the verge', it is more than tempting to assume that Davies knew the early meaning of 'verge' as 'the space within a boundary' that allows for movement. The word is used in this sense in Thomas Gray's 'The Bard', which is not only anthologized in Palgrave's *Golden Treasury*, the favourite book of one of Karen's nurses, but also deals with themes close to Davies's romantic Welsh ones. Even without this knowledge, the river as an image implies a fluid border, and, as Karen gazes into it, her face merges with its swaying, flowing and transmuting movements. Paradoxically, as all identities negotiated along the borders of culture must be paradoxical, Karen's identity achieves an organic mobility that cannot be dissolved.

It is not too morbid to read this final death in Davies's fiction in positive and liberating terms. In fact, it is appropriate that an author obsessively concerned with death and its paraphernalia should close with death as a satisfying release. Karen's death seems like more of a sleep, a daily oblivion that Davies himself looked forward to with rapturous abandon. It is also appropriate that, with death, we end as we began. One of the recurring motifs in *Honeysuckle Girl* is the Lazarus motif, which refers not only to Anna Kavan's collection of short stories, *I Am Lazarus* (1945), but to Davies's long-standing negotiation of identity from beneath the death-dealing repression of sexual prudery. As we have seen, in *Rings on Her Fingers*, Edith Roberts felt her 'mind was turning into a slab of stone, her soul petrifying within her' (Davies, 1930a: 15), but in *Count Your Blessings*, Jane rises sensually from beneath her father's 'grave' (Davies, 1932: 8) reading of the story of Lazarus, her 'bosom issu[ing] from her narrow waist like a white hyacinth breaking from its sheath; her white legs, freed of her flannel petticoats . . . stretch[ing] and kick[ing] with a nervous joy' (ibid.).

Conclusion

Davies died of lung cancer on 21 August, 1978 in St Pancras Hospital. Throughout his long career, he wrote over twenty novels, two plays, a biography, two books on Wales and over a hundred short stories in periodicals and collections, in addition to various essays, reviews and broadcasts. One can hardly grasp the range of theme and tone across such a vibrant and complex career. In this study, whole novels and dozens of stories have sadly fallen by the wayside, leaving significant topics and significant aspects of Davies's life largely unaddressed. We have not lingered on Davies's Henley stories, neither have we engaged to any great extent the discussion of his racial representations, nor have we examined his exploitation of and appeal to the American reading public, nor have we wondered at his consistently thwarted efforts to write for the silver screen. Perhaps this can be forgiven in the case of an author who wrote fiction for over half a century, between 1926 and 1978. Yet this span of years reminds us that Davies's stories and novels provide irreplaceable insights into the changing social, political and economic conditions in which he wrote. His career also illuminates the changing conditions of publishing and authorship, which, coupled with the changing political contexts, had a great deal of influence on the negotiation of his professional and personal identity as a gay Welsh London artist from working-class south Wales.

This book has examined how the major shifts in Davies's life and career occurred along the boundaries of a carefully negotiated identity, and the process has illustrated an unmistakable transformation of a young and struggling highbrow writer in the leftist coteries between the wars into a postmodern writer of crime and deviance on the borders of policed identities. Throughout this transformation, however, Davies remained committed to certain abiding themes that the changing demands of the market obscured and obstructed, but never completely silenced. Davies was always the defender of the independent and visionary artist who defied limited definitions of gender, attacked middle-class domestic respectability, dismissed national borders and subverted forms of policing and surveillance. This defiant posture is all part of Davies's commitment to his 'own interior liberty', which I like to think he achieved, despite his financial instability, despite his dependence upon the literary market, and in spite of the silence imposed upon his sexual identity.

When Davies began his career by changing his name and writing in the style of Caradoc Evans, adding, as he claimed 'a Welsh leek' to The Progressive Bookshop coterie, he launched his career along well-trodden paths of the literary market. For at least the first half of this career, a large part of his appeal and its endurance derived from writing about Wales for an English audience that had a taste for literature dealing with their alien little neighbours, especially if it was romantic and exotic, a little scandalous, or black with miners. It was in this vein that Heinemann took Davies on, and in this vein that they tried to keep him, despite Davies's growing discomfort with the dubious aesthetic achievement of being a marketable Welsh writer.

For many, writing about the Welsh in the 1920s and 1930s meant writing about the working class. Therefore, in the hard years leading up to the Second World War, when south Wales was one of the bleakest regions in Britain, readers turned to writers like Davies. Davies's relationship to these working communities was conflicted and complex. Politically, his sympathies were with the miners, but artistically, he resented 'the growls and barking people seem[ed] to expect of [him] as a Welsh novelist' (RD to GHW 3 May 1935 HRHRC).

While it may have been difficult to cope with the expectations that Davies's market had of his Welsh and working-class themes, it was almost impossible to cope with his sexual themes in a way that made sense of his gay experience. Davies never felt that it was his job to write an 'unfrightened' homosexual novel that reflected his own experience. Nevertheless, every stage of Davies's life and career was deeply implicated in his gay identity. Much of Davies's fiction obliquely redefines the parameters of Welshness to replace its 'internal territory' with its 'internal difference'. In such a Wales, where identities come into being only along the borders, a queer subjectivity materializes as an integral part of Welsh identity throughout the twentieth century. In Davies, therefore, we have a gay history that is legible even in conditions that were so completely hostile to its expression. The insidious forms of that hostility eventually emerged as the primary concern of Davies's later fiction, which may be read as an extended attack on the forms of surveillance that police the borders of the 'proper' and the 'perverse'.

One wonders what Davies would think of twenty-first-century Wales, where a queer identity has begun to emerge in the post-devolution commitment to broadly defined human rights. In 2001, the Welsh Assembly Government oversaw the establishment of the Lesbian, Gay and Bisexual (LGB) Forum Cymru, which became Stonewall Cymru in 2003, marking the political awakening of both the LGB and non-gay communities across Wales in the early years of this decade (Jones, 2008). It is therefore appropriate that Davies was officially honoured by Wales both before and after his death. In 1971, he was awarded the Welsh Arts Council Prize for his lifetime of literary work, and in 1991, the Rhys Davies Trust established the Rhys Davies Short Story Competition. Most recently, Parthian published a new edition of *The Withered Root* in 2007, eighty years after its first publication. Davies's embeddedness in the literary establishment of Wales is now certain, as is playfully evident in Rachel Trezise's recent story 'Fresh Apples', which includes a character who has been named Rhys Davies 'after some gay Welsh poet' (Trezise, 2005: 3).

Davies now occupies an honoured place in the official culture of the Welsh arts in a century where new gay Welsh voices have arisen. Writers like John Sam Jones and Roger Williams, for example, were certainly possible without Davies, but Davies provides an important context of a long history dealing with similar questions of queer national belonging. When reading Jones, for instance, it is very hard not to hear Davies's familiar agonized longing for home. In *With Angels and Furies*, a young gay man reflects on the storied landscape seen outside the window of a bus as he travels to his parents' home:

> Winding along the Dee, with no other passengers to protest about gnats or the freshening breeze from the open windows, he enjoyed the hilly countryside. Reminiscent of a childhood landscape that was locked somewhere deep in his psyche, the contours and textures of the land released inside him a sense of wellbeing and he was embraced by belonging. The yellows and the purples of gorse and heather flared up, vivid in the setting sun's furnace, and fierce blue-black shadows swathed the hollows, casting them into timeless mystery. It was an ancient land of myths and legends that had borne him, in territories that Idris had tyrannized from his craggy, summit throne and where beasts like *yr afanc* lurked, deep in the crystal clarity of the valley lakes. But, then, the chain of lonely villages strung out along the hillside triggered only anxieties that sapped the mawkish belonging that had seeped through his senses. As he passed through each community, a profound estrangement engulfed him and sucked him to the edge of the familiar, dreadful mire that seemed always to beckon from some cavern even deeper inside his soul. (Jones, 2005: 38–9)

One can hardly question Davies's relevance to the continuing story of Wales, for, clearly, even today, gay Welsh writers grapple with the challenges of articulating themselves on the borders of the past and the present, belonging and estrangement, self and home.

Bibliography

Primary sources

Davies, Rhys (1997). *Print of a Hare's Foot: An Autobiographical Beginning* (Bridgend: Seren).
—— (1996a). *Rhys Davies: Collected Stories*, vol. 1, ed. Meic Stephens (Llandysul: Gomer).
—— (1996b). *Rhys Davies: Collected Stories*, vol. 2, ed. Meic Stephens (Llandysul: Gomer), pp. 93–104.
—— (1996c). *Rhys Davies: Collected Stories*, vol. 3, ed. Meic Stephens (Llandysul: Gomer).
—— (1996d). *Ram with Red Horns* (Bridgend: Seren).
—— (1975). *Honeysuckle Girl* (London: Heinemann).
—— (1971). *Nobody Answered the Bell* (London: Heinemann).
—— (1960). *Girl Waiting in the Shade* (London: Heinemann).
—— (1958). 'Our contributors: No. 1 Rhys Davies', *Wales* (September), 7.
—— (1957). *The Perishable Quality* (London: Heinemann).
—— (1955). 'Preface', *Collected Stories of Rhys Davies* (London: Heinemann).
—— (1954). *The Painted King* (London: Heinemann).
—— (1951). *Marianne* (London: Heinemann).
—— (1946a). 'From my notebook (III)', *Wales*, 22, 13–19.
—— (1946b). *The Dark Daughters* (London: Heinemann).
—— (1946c). 'Reply to questionnaire', *Wales*, 22, 18–19.
—— (1946d). 'Time and the Welsh mountains', in Richard Harman (ed.), *Countryside Character* (London: Blandford Press), pp. 209–19.
—— (1944a). *The Black Venus* (London: Heinemann).
—— (1944b). 'From a notebook', *Wales*, 2nd ser., 4, 5, 64–70.
—— (1943a). 'From my notebook', in *Wales*, 2, 10–12.
—— (1943b). *The Story of Wales* (London: Collins).
—— (1941). *Tomorrow to Fresh Woods* (London: Heinemann).
—— (1940a). *Under the Rose*, London, Heinemann.

—— (1940b). 'People of Britain', BBC broadcast, Overseas Central Transmission, Part 1, 3 November, 1940, 3.45–4.00 p.m.
—— (1938). *Jubilee Blues* (London and Toronto: Heinemann).
—— (1937a). *My Wales* (London: Jarrolds).
—— (1937b). *A Time to Laugh* (London: Heinemann).
—— (1935). *Honey and Bread* (London: Putnam).
—— (1933a). *The Red Hills* (New York: Covici Friede).
—— (1933b, as Owen Pitman). *Two Loves I Have* (London: Jonathan Cape).
—— (1932). *Count Your Blessings* (London: Putnam).
—— (1931). 'Writing about the Welsh', in John Gawsworth (ed.), *Ten Contemporaries: Notes Toward Their Definitive Bibliography* (London: Benn Limited).
—— (1930a). *Rings on Her Fingers* (London: Shaylor).
—— (1930b). *The Stars, the World, and the Women* (London: Jackson).
—— (1927). 'Mr Rhys Davies and Welsh dialogue', *Western Mail* (30 November), 9, C.
—— (1927a). 'Crude phases of Welsh life', *Western Mail* (1 February).
—— (1927b). *The Withered Root* (London: Robert Holden).
—— (1927c). *The Song of Songs and Other Stories* (London: Archer).

Secondary sources

Aaron, Jane (1995a). 'A national seduction: Wales in nineteenth-century women's writing', *New Welsh Review*, 27, 31–8.
—— (1995b) 'The hoydens of wild Wales: representations of women in Victorian and Edwardian fiction', Welsh Writing in English, 1, 23–39.
'A novel of Wales. Strange people and bad dialogue', *Western Mail*, (24 November 1927).
'Aberpennar, Davies' [Pennar Davies] (1946). 'Anti-nationalism among the Anglo-Welsh', *The Welsh Nationalist* (February 1946), 8.
Baker, Denys Val (1952). 'Man from the valley', *John O'London's Weekly* (24 October), 61, 1476, 1–2.
Beddoe, Deirdre (2000). *Out of the Shadows: A History of Women in Twentieth-Century Wales* (Cardiff: University of Wales Press).
Bhabha, Homi K. (1994). *The Location of Culture* (London: Routledge).
Bohata, Kirsti (2001). 'The black Venus: atavistic sexualities', in Meic Stephens (ed.), *Rhys Davies: Decoding the Hare* (Cardiff: University of Wales Press), pp. 231–43.

Brown, Tony. (2001). '"The memory of lost countries": Rhys Davies's Wales', in Meic Stephens (ed.), *Rhys Davies: Decoding the Hare* (Cardiff: University of Wales Press), pp. 71–86.
Callard, D. A. (1994). 'Rhys Davies', *Dictionary of Literary Biography: British Short Fiction Writers, 1945–1980* (Detroit: Gale Research).
—— (1992), *The Case of Anna Kavan* (London: Peter Owen).
—— (1991), 'Rhys Davies and the Welsh expatriate novel', *Planet*, 89, 84–7.
Caspary, Vera (1957). *Laura* (New York: Dell Publishing Company).
'Corroboration of W.J.'s contention' (1927). *Western Mail* (8 December).
Croft-Cooke, Rupert (1963). *The Numbers Came* (London: Putnam).
Dixon, Michael J. (2001). 'The epic Rhondda: romanticism and realism in the Rhondda trilogy', in Meic Stephens (ed.), *Rhys Davies: Decoding the Hare* (Cardiff: University of Wales Press), pp. 40–53.
Edwards, John (1937). Review of *A Time to Laugh*, in *Life and Letters Today* (Summer), 16, 8, 157.
Foucault, Michel (1990). *The History of Sexuality: An Introduction*, vol. 1 (New York: Vintage).
Fox, R. M. (1938). *Smokey Crusade* (London: Hogarth Press).
Garman, Douglas (1935). 'A revolutionary writer', *Welsh Review* (June), 1, 5, 263–7.
George, Daniel (1941). 'Welshman's bait', review of *Tomorrow to Fresh Woods* by Rhys Davies, *Mr. Bunting at War* by Robert Greenwood, *To Sing with the Angels* by Maurice Hindus, *Conquer* by John Masefield, *The Remarkable Andrew* by Dalton Trumbo, *No Time for To-day* by Adeline Rumsey, *City of Illusion* by Vardis Fisher, *Beckoning Ridge* by Emerson Waldman, in *Tribune* (14 November), 16–17.
—— (1940). 'Under the Welsh rose', review of *Under the Rose* by Rhys Davies, *Tribune* (27 September), 22.
Gramich, Katie (2001). 'The masquerade of gender in the stories of Rhys Davies', in Meic Stephen (ed.), *Rhys Davies: Decoding the Hare* (Cardiff: University of Wales Press), 205–15.
Hanley, James (1931). *The German Prisoner* (London: Charles Lahr).
—— (1990). *Boy* (London: A. Deutsch).
'Hard Times' (1941). Review of *Tomorrow to Fresh Woods* by Rhys Davies, *Times Literary Supplement* (25 October), 529.
Hopkins, Kenneth (1954). *The Corruption of a Poet* (London: James Barrie).
Horsley, Lee (2005). *Twentieth-Century Crime Fiction* (Oxford: Oxford University Press).
Houlbrook, Matthew (2005). *Queer London: Perils and Pleasures in the Sexual Metropolis, 1918–1957* (Chicago: Chicago University Press).
J.W. (1927). 'Welsh dialect in "The Withered Root". Testing the literal translation', *Western Mail* (8 December).

John, Angela (ed.) (1991). *Our Mothers' Land: Chapters in Welsh Women's History, 1830–1939* (Cardiff: University of Wales Press).
Jones, Bill, and Chris Williams (1999). *B. L. Coombes* (Cardiff: University of Wales Press).
Jones, Glyn (1996). 'Every genuine writer finds his own Wales', in *New Welsh Review* (Winter), 9, 3, 11–15.
Jones, John Sam (2008). 'Coming out of the Welsh Dresser (Closet) – The politics of being out and proud since devolution in 1997', paper presented as part of the Queer Wales Panel at the 2008 International Conference on Welsh Studies, University of Toronto, 31 July–2 August.
—— (2005). *With Angels and Furies* (London: Gay Men's Press).
Jones, Lewis (2006). *Cwmardy and We Live* (Cardigan: Parthian).
Jones, Owen Vernon (1991). *Porth County: The School and its Boys* (Gregalow: Hackman Printers).
Jones, T. Gwynn (1927). 'The withered root controversy. Cymricized English picturesque', *Western Mail* (10 December).
—— (1927). 'English as spoken in Wales. The dialogue in "The Withered Root"', *Western Mail* (3 December).
Knight, Stephen (2001). '"Not a place for me": Rhys Davies's fiction and the coal industry', in Meic Stephens (ed.), *Rhys Davies: Decoding the Hare* (Cardiff: University of Wales Press), pp. 54–70.
Lewis, Saunders (1939). *Is there an Anglo-Welsh literature?* (Cardiff: Guild of Welsh Graduates).
McCracken, Scott. (1998). *Pulp: Reading Popular Fiction* (Manchester: Manchester University Press).
Mégroz, R. L. (1932). *Rhys Davies: A Critical Sketch* (London, W. & G. Foyle Limited).
Miller, D. A. (1988). *The Novel and the Police* (Berkeley: University of California Press).
Mitchell, J. Lawrence (2001). '"I wish I had a trumpet": Rhys Davies and the creative impulse', in Meic Stephens (ed.), *Rhys Davies: Decoding the Hare* (Cardiff: University of Wales Press), 147–61.
—— (1998). 'Home and abroad: The dilemma of Rhys Davies', *Planet*, 70, 78–90.
Morson, Gary Saul, and Caryl Emerson (1990). *Mikhail Bakhtin: Creation of a Prosaics* (Stanford: Stanford University Press).
O'Brien, Kate (1940). Review of *Under the Rose* by Rhys Davies, *Spectator* (4 October), 347–8.
Osborne, Huw. (2008) '"What a fine body of men they are": class, gender, and sexuality in the authorial identity of Rhys Davies', *Almanac: Yearbook of Welsh Writing in English*, 12, 192–227.

Pritchett, V. S. (1937). 'Political novels', review of *Death Without Battle* by Ludwig Renn, *Mean Without Mercy* by Alfred Döblin, *A Time to Laugh* by Rhys Davies, *The Labour Leader* by Gabrielle Vallings, *The Savage Days* by Phillip Toynbee, *New Statesman and Nation* (13 March), 428.
Prys-Williams, Barbara (2001). 'Rhys Davies as autobiographer: hare or Houdini?' Rhys Davies's Wales', in Meic Stephens (ed.), *Rhys Davies: Decoding the Hare* (Cardiff: University of Wales Press), pp. 104–37.
R.J. (1930) Review of *Rings on her Fingers* by Rhys Davies. *New Republic* (10 September), 108.
Review of *Rings on Her Fingers* by Rhys Davies (1930). *Times Literary Supplement* (August), 642.
Review of *Under the Rose* (1940). *Times Literary Supplement* (21 September), 481.
Rhydderch, Francesca (1997). 'Dual nationality, divided identity: ambivalent narratives of Britishness in the Welsh novels of Anna Maria Bennett', *Welsh Writing in English*, 3, 1–17.
Roberts, Glyn (1936). 'They interpret Wales – In English', *Western Mail* (28 July).
Scaggs, John (2005). *Crime Fiction* (New York: Routledge).
Sedgwick, Eve Kosofsky (1990). *Epistemology of the Closet* (Berkeley: University of California Press).
—— (1985). *Between Men: English Literature and Male Homosocial Desire* (New York: Columbia University Press).
Sinfield, Alan (1994). *The Wilde Century: Effeminacy, Oscar Wilde and the Queer Moment* (London: Cassell).
Smith, Dai (2001). 'Rhys Davies and his "turbulent valley"', in Meic Stephens (ed.), *Rhys Davies: Decoding the Hare* (Cardiff: University of Wales Press), pp. 29–39.
—— (1999). *Wales: A Question for History* (Bridgend: Seren).
Spender, Stephen (1934). 'By the lake', *New Stories*, 1, 1, 52–80.
Stephens, Meic (ed.) (2001), *Decoding the Hare* (Cardiff: University of Wales Press).
Thomas, M. Wynn (1999). *Corresponding Cultures: The Two Literatures of Wales* (Cardiff: University of Wales Press).
—— (1997). '"Never seek to tell thy love": Rhys Davies's fiction', *Welsh Writing in English*, 3, 1–21.
—— (1992). *Internal Difference: Literature in 20th-Century Wales* (Cardiff: University of Wales Press).
Trezise, Rachel (2005). 'Fresh Apples', *Fresh Apples* (Cardigan: Parthian).
'Welsh Tales', (1942). Review of *A Finger in Every Pie* by Rhys Davies, *Times Literary Supplement* (12 September), 449.

West, G. H. (1936). Review of *The Things Men Do* by Rhys Davies, *Times Literary Supplement* (4 July), 562.

—— (1932). Review of *The Red Hills* by Rhys Davies, *Times Literary Supplement* (15 December), 960.

Wilde, Oscar (2002). 'The decay of lying', David Damrosh et al. (eds), *The Longman Anthology of British Literature*, vol. 2 (New York: Longman).

Williams, Daniel (2001). 'Withered roots: ideas of race in the writings of Rhys Davies and D. H. Lawrence', in Meic Stephens (ed.), *Rhys Davies: Decoding the Hare* (Cardiff: University of Wales Press), pp. 87–103.

Williams, Michael (2003). *Ivor Novello: Screen Idol* (London: British Film Institute).

Williams, Raymond (1980). 'The Welsh industrial novel', *Problems in Materialism and Culture* (London: Verso), pp. 213–29.

'Woman of Wales' (1938). Review of *Jubilee Blues* by Rhys Davies, *Times Literary Supplement* (15 October), 659.

Index

Aaron 29
Aaron, Jane 74, 76
'Abraham's Glory' 108
aestheticism / dandyism 17–25, 54, 77, 95, 118–21, 128
art 97–8, 124–5;
  and consumer culture 51
  and class *see* aestheticism / dandyism *and* industrialism / industrial fiction
  and market 26, 30–3, 35, 62, 96–9
  and sexuality *see* aestheticism / dandyism
  and Welshness 96–99
Ashleigh, Charlie 35

Bakhtin, Mikhail 2–3
Bates, H. E. 29–30
Beddoe, Deirdre 11
Bennett, Anna Maria 74
Bennett, Arnold 63
Bhabha, Homi K. 2
Black Venus, The 80–5, 89, 99, 101
Bohata, Kirsti 76, 81
'Boy with a Trumpet' 89–90
Brown, Tony 76, 82
Bullock, George 31, 86

Caspary, Vera 114–16
Chatto & Windus 32
Chekhov, Anton 62
'Cherry-Blossom on the Rhine' 94–5
'Chosen One, The' 116
colonialism 5, 43–6, 70–1, 76, 81–3
Coombes, B. L. 59
Count Your Blessings 14, 41, 58, 131

crime fiction 104–5, 112–22
Croft-Cooke, Rupert 29–30
Cunard, Nancy 81

dandyism / aestheticism 17–25, 54, 77, 95, 118–21, 128
Dark Daughters, The 99, 101
Davies, Pennar 36–7
Davies, Rhys
  authorial identity 26–7, 30–2, 35–7, 50, 58–67, 96–103
  bachelorhood 106–12, 125
  childhood and youth 7–15, 18–25
  class identity 2–11, 26–9, 35, 50, 52–3, 58–64;
  critical reception 36–8, 41–2, 58–64, 85–7, 101
  marketing 36–9, 62, 98–102
  nationalism / anti-nationalism 39–46, 68–75, 82–3
  readership 26–9, 36–46, 62
  sexual identity 2–6, 11, 15–25, 33, 50, 54–7, 76–83, 93–4, 104–22, 126–9 133–5
  travels 4, 26, 32–5, 50, 64, 69–71, 84, 93–4
  Welsh identity 2–6, 39–42, 68–75, 96–103
  see also titles of works
Dixon, Michael J. 60–1
'Doctor's Wife, The' 126–9

Earp, T. W. 29
Eliot, T. S. 97
Evans, Caradoc 29, 97, 133
Evans, A. Dwye 100–1

Index

Fabes, Gilbert 7, 31
fascism 92–5
Foucault, Michel 4, 112
Fox, R. M. 30

George, Daniel 86–7
Gibbings, Robert 31
'Gift of Death' 46–7
Girl Waiting in the Shade 70
Gollancz 32
Glan Ystrad trilogy 58, 60
  see also entries for *Honey and Bread, A Time to Laugh* and *Jubilee Blues*
Golden Cockerel Press 31
Gramich, Katie 55
Green, Russell 29
Gyde, Arnold 99–101

Hall, Radclyffe 105
Hanley, James 105
Heinemann 36, 70, 98–101, 133
Henderson, Philip 31
'History' 43–6
homosexuality 3–4, 15–25, 33, 50, 76–83, 93–4, 104–22, 126–9, 133–5
homosociality 54–7
Honey and Bread 31, 58, 60, 71–80, 83, 85, 127
Honeysuckle Girl 123–7, 129–31
Hopkins, Kenneth 29–30
Horsley, Lee 113–14
Houlbrook, Matt 106–7
Huxley, Aldous 29

industrialism / industrial fiction 43, 51–3, 58–69, 75, 100–1
'Interlude' 27, 51

James, Hanley 97
John, Angela 11
Jones, Glyn 59, 97
Jones, Gwyn 59
Jones, Jack 58, 97
Jones, John Sam 135
Jones, Lewis 8, 58–60
Jubilee Blues 54–6, 58, 60, 62–3, 68–9, 80, 85

Kavan, Anna 104, 131

Knight, Stephen 58

Lahr, Charles 12, 26, 29–30, 32–3, 35, 67, 84, 96, 105, 109, 129
Lawrence, D. H. 27, 29, 33, 47, 50, 81, 89, 105, 109
Llewellyn, Richard 8, 75

McCracken, Scott 113
McLeod, Fiona 86
Marianne 101, 116
Marriott, Raymond 31, 64–5, 70, 85–6, 88
Masculinity 11–12, 18–19, 54–7
Maupassant, Guy de 62
Mégroz, R. L. 13
Melville, Herman 86
middlebrow culture 43, 47–9, 51, 53–4
Miller, D. A. 113
misogyny 5, 46–50, 53–4, 78
Mitchell, J. Lawrence 20, 29
Mosley, Oswald 93
'Mrs Evans Number Six' 47–9, 53
My Wales 39–41, 70, 101

Nepean, Mary Edith 36
New Coterie, The 28–31
'Nightgown' 54, 65
Nobody Answered the Bell 116, 121–4
noir 113–15
Nonconformity 5, 10–11, 13–15, 25, 37, 43, 46–7, 50, 75–6
Novello, Ivor 100, 110

O'Brien, Kate 86
O'Flaherty, Liam 29
'On the Tip' 65–7

Painted King, The 100–1, 103, 110–12, 119, 127
Perishable Quality, The 70, 100–3, 116
'Pits are at the Top, The' 65
police/policing 104, 106, 112–21, 125
Powys, T. F. 29
Print of a Hare's Foot 4–5, 10–12, 17–19, 21–5, 70, 93, 108–9, 111, 126
Pritchett, V. S. 63
Progressive Bookshop, The 29–30, 67, 84, 96, 105, 133

Prys-Williams, Barbara 17, 111
Putnam 32

Quinain, Louis 35, 85, 96, 114

race 2, 40, 70–1, 76, 81–2
Raine, Allen 36, 74
Ram with Red Horns 116, 124
Rhydderch, Francesca 76
Rhys, Keidrych 97
Rings on her Fingers 13–14, 20–1, 37, 54, 58, 131
'Romantic Policewoman, The' 116–18
Red Hills, The 50–1, 53–4, 56–7, 61
Roberts, Glyn 36
Roberts, William 29

Scaggs, John 114
Second World War 84–95
Sedgwick, Eve Kosofsky 16, 54, 106–7
Selver, Paul 29
Sinfield, Alan 19–20, 23
'Sisters, The' 27
'Skull, The' 31
Smith, Dai 1–2, 16, 67
Spectator, The 86
'Spectre de la Rose' 90–2
Spender, Stephen 77
Song of Songs and Other Stories 29
'Stars, the World, and the Women, The' 47
Stonewall 105
Story of Wales, The 37–8, 69, 82–3

Tale 29
Taylor, Louise 104

Thomas, Dylan 103
Thomas, Gwyn 59
Thomas, M. Wynn 2, 56
'Time and the Welsh Mountains' 69–71
Time to Laugh, A 51–3, 58, 60, 63, 74–5, 80, 85
Times Literary Supplement 61–3
Tomorrow to Fresh Woods 8–10, 17–18, 21–4, 26, 51, 55, 60, 64–5, 87–88, 99
Tolstoy, Leo 63
Trezise, Rachel 134
Tribune, The 86
'Two Friends, The' 65

Under the Rose 60, 85–7, 89, 95, 104, 113, 116, 122
Urquhart, Fred 109–10, 112

Wales 17
Wells, Vincent 33, 85, 96, 109
Welsh language 40
Welsh Nationalist 36–7
West, G. H. 31, 61–3, 76
Western Mail 36, 42, 64
'Wigs, Costumes, Masks' 109, 112, 118–21, 126–7
Wilde, Oscar 23–5, 119
Williams, Daniel 76
Williams, Roger 135
Williams, Raymond 69
Williams, Michael 110
Withered Root, The 13–14, 26, 29, 32, 58, 134
Wolfendon Report 104–5
'Writing about the Welsh' 42